Praise for *Who am I?*

"One of the most inspiring and life changing stories you will ever experience. And for me, it was just the beginning of so much more..."

Candice Alger, CEO Giant Studios - recent film work: Avatar, Tintin, Real Steel

"...healing does occur, and that's why your story is so important to those who confront the demons that you took on – and defeated."

Professor Volney P. Gay, Director of Psychotherapy Training Vanderbilt University and Director of the Center for the Study of Religion and Culture

"As to O'Connor—I'm editing a book on her right now, so forgive the long quote—but she cited St. Cyril of Jerusalem, in instructing catechumens, who wrote: 'The dragon sits by the side of the road, watching those who pass. Beware lest he devour you. We go to the Father of Souls, but it is necessary to pass by the dragon." Explaining that passage and her own calling as a writer, O'Connor stated: "No matter what form the dragon may take, it is of this mysterious passage past him, or into his jaws, that stories of any depth will always be concerned to tell, and this being the case, it requires considerable courage at any time, in any century, not to turn away from the storyteller.'

Silouan, you are such a storyteller, and I for one will not turn away from you."

Jon Peede, Publisher at Virginia Quarterly Review and Former Director of Literature, Grants Director, National Endowment for the Arts

WHO AM I?

or how I learned to fly with angels

The Incredible Story of a Broken Man's Desperate
Struggle to find Love, Meaning, and Purpose

by Silouan Green
Copyright © 2013 Everon LLC
Visit **www.silouan.com** for more from Silouan
facebook.com/silouangreen and twitter.com/silouangreen

For:
For my wife Thecla and my seven dear children: Isaac, Mary
Inger, Irene Dare, Jude, Maximus, Georgia, and Gabriel – you
suffered with me, and we share the glory together.

Dr. Gia Lanzano – you saved my life.

Kingsville, Texas, and everyone there who gave me
encouragement.

Dr. Volney Gay – you taught me to ask the right questions. It
made all the difference.

My dear friends, Jim Seabury and Madison Perkins, whose
unwavering belief and support helped make all this possible.

© 2009 Everon LLC

First Printing - 2009
Second Printing - 2010
Third Printing - 2012
Fourth Printing - 2013

ISBN13: 978-0615720913
ISBN10: 0615720919

Quantity orders and not-for-profit book rates available,
info@everoninc.com.

WHO AM I?

It was dark, hot, and damp. The hood over my head blocked any light except that glowing from the backlit dials and switches. A storm was coming, and the air hung thick with moisture. Sweat dripped from my forehead down into my eyes, but the glare shield of the flight helmet kept my gloved hands from wiping them. I was uncomfortable, and everything was shaking.

Ten thousand pounds of thrust burned beneath me – twenty tons of metal groaned with the strain. The air conditioner wouldn't kick in until we were churning more air, so I sat in this furnace struggling to remain alert. Soon I would be accelerating without sight to over three hundred miles per hour. Everything seemed to check out fine, but I was scared. Of course, I was always scared.

We were off, Lieutenant Skinner and I, into a storm we thought we could evade. But the storm wasn't the problem. Our problem was the fire — and the blinking lights and my paralyzed mind.

"Lieutenant Skinner, help me! Help me!" I waited to die.

And then my seat exploded, and I left the fire and the dying groaning metal. The air hit me like a wall, and I felt my body scream, and pull, and tear. I saw Lieutenant Skinner go by.

He was thrown toward a line of trees, and then I blacked out.

I woke on my back, and Lieutenant Skinner was dead.

And the soul stays when the child fades away.

CHOICES

As far as Samuel could see there were no trees – just rocks, hills, streams, green grass, sheep, and the Atlantic Ocean. He climbed atop a boulder the size of a Honda Civic and sat down to be alone with it all. He was an exchange student in Iceland.

Samuel had awoke around 2:00 a.m. and looked out his bedroom window to see the sun hanging on the horizon. Unable to sleep, he took his first late-night walk up a grassy hill overlooking the fjord behind the home of his host family. Samuel was living on a sheep farm on the north coast of Iceland, and his nearest neighbor was three miles away via a narrow, hilly, and winding gravel road.

It was the middle of summer, but the night breeze chilled the temperature to the upper thirties as Samuel clenched his arms trying to stay warm. From his hilltop boulder, he could see for miles in every direction – across the hay fields, across the valleys, across the ocean that spread wide in front of him. The glow of the hanging sun gave everything a halo of burnt gold, and the sky was a smooth gradient of blue to black.

"So, what's in store for me?" he spoke out loud, pondering what he thought was a bright future. When he returned home to Indiana in a few months he would be a senior in high school, and he was excited. Slated to be captain of the basketball team, his girlfriend would be the pom-pom captain, and he would finally be the "big man" on the campus of Lagrange High School.

"Ain't that funny," he pondered. He could remember moving all those years ago, just a picked-on preacher's kid in a new school. Well, he had shown them. Now he was tall, athletic, and one of the most popular kids in school.

"Samuel, you will suffer." A deep voice erupted from the sky. Samuel jumped up, looking around for the intruder. He could not see anyone, and the voice continued.

"You will eventually do much good, Samuel, but first you must suffer."

"You will suffer, you will suffer, you will..." The voice echoed and trailed off in the windy night air.

"What?" Samuel screamed. Had he really heard that voice?

"Who are you, what do you want?" he questioned.

"Hey!!!!!!" Samuel yelled, but all he heard was the blowing wind and a few seagulls riding the night breeze.

Shaking, Samuel waited all night to hear the voice again. Actually, he waited all summer. And while he waited, he began to write prodigiously. Poems mostly, something he had not done since childhood. He would sit on the boulder every day for hours, writing poems, dreaming of how he would change the world. As the days in Iceland passed by, Samuel changed, and he was happier. He let his hair grow, pierced his ears, worked out, and made merry with fellow exchange students from France, Germany, and around the world. He had never felt so much joy and freedom. But he still could not forget the words:

"Samuel, you will suffer."

A few months later Samuel was back home in the States, and he was the talk of the school. He had left for Iceland the picture of a middle-American schoolboy – a churchgoing, blond-haired, blue-eyed, clean-cut, intelligent sports star; he returned looking like some European exchange student with pierced ears, torn jeans, colorful shirts, and dirty, long hair. He shared his poems with whomever would listen, and he even thought about buying a guitar and putting them to music. And then Ron James, head basketball coach, asked him into his office.

"Samuel," Coach James caught Samuel in the hallway. "I need to see you a minute in my office."

"Sure, coach," he answered.

Coach James was about six feet five inches and walked with an awkward gait. The expression on his face was dour, to say the least. As Samuel followed him down the hall, fear grew inside him.

They entered his office. Coach shut the door, and Samuel took a chair in the front row of seats as Coach James sat on his desk. He got right to the point.

"Samuel, I gotta say, what the hell is with the earring, crazy clothes, and long hair? I'm counting on you this year." He was mad, and he was looking at Samuel with great consternation.

"Whad'ya mean, Coach?" Samuel uncomfortably questioned. "Just something I did in Iceland. What's the big deal?" This was the wrong answer.

"Big deal?" Coach James bellowed. "You look like some fag. You're supposed to be our captain this year. Practice starts in two weeks." He paused, and Samuel kept his mouth shut.

"I'll make it easy for you," he continued. "You lose the earring, tattered clothes, and long hair, and I forget about this. You'll still be captain, and we'll have a great year. You don't lose this crap, forget about being captain, and I'll find some reason to kick you off the team."

Samuel stared at him blankly.

"It's your decision. I don't want to see this junk tomorrow." And with that he left the room, taking the air with him.

Samuel's chest heaved as his head split. "You bastard," he

hissed to the empty office.

But then five minutes later it got worse, and Samuel remembered the words, "You will suffer."

As he walked down the hallway to his locker, his girlfriend Angie approached with a glum look. "What the hell?" Samuel thought, "What now?"

"We need to talk, Samuel," she said almost under her breath.

"Sure," he replied, and they ducked into an empty classroom.

"What's up?" he asked as they entered. He tried to grab her hand but she pulled away.

"We just need to talk," she repeated.

"Maybe we do." Samuel considered. "It's been hard talking to you since I got back."

Angie didn't reply. She played with her hands and stared at the ground.

"C'mon, Angie," Samuel goaded, "you asked me in here. What's going on?"

"Well, I can't see you anymore, Samuel," she answered icily as the room became cold steel.

"What, what are you talking about?" Samuel panicked. "What about all those letters you sent while I was gone? You said you loved me. You said you were waiting for me."

"But you changed – you, you're kinda weird." She looked down again.

"Weird? You told me I looked cool; you told me I was different and it turned you on."

He tried to grab her hand and she pulled away again. "Please, please, Angie. Please, I'll quit wearing this and go back to normal."

"It's not just that, Samuel. I'm seeing someone."

"Seeing someone! Who? I'll beat his ass!" Samuel quivered.

"He doesn't go to school here. He's in college."

"College," Samuel's voice squeaked. "What's his name?" Her answer was a dagger.

"Todd Pontius," she answered shortly.

"Todd Pontius. His brother plays for the Chicago Bears," Samuel stammered for an answer. "You, you whore." And with that Samuel stormed out of the room as Angie began to sob.

That night Samuel sat in his room staring into an abyss. He was pushed in a corner and just wanted the pain to go away. He wanted to be "the man" again. So he took out the earring, threw away the torn jeans, ripped up his poems, and flushed the scraps down the toilet. He even took some scissors and cut his own hair. Then he fell to his pillow and cried. He would survive his senior year, but every day would feel like he was walking in someone else's shoes.

"You will suffer." The voice would not cease to echo.

That was high school; this was college. Samuel had returned for his second semester at Vanderbilt University in Nashville, Tennessee. The first had been a success. He had earned As and one B, and had rediscovered the beauty of creativity in freshman writing class. It was invigorating. His possibilities seemed endless, and he thought about conquering the world again. It seemed clear Samuel would major in psychology or religion while beginning again to follow his creative muse.

But walking into his dorm with a load of new textbooks the day before classes, he came across a sign that would change his life. It was a Marine Corps officer recruiting poster that expounded on the opportunities in the United States Marine Corps to be a fighter pilot. It excited him, and he began to remember youthful dreams of flying jet aircraft. He could be a tough Marine to boot.

Fueled by youthful enthusiasm, that very next day Samuel walked into the recruiting office, and before he really knew what he was doing, as happens to young men, he signed the papers. The two following summers would be spent attending Officer Candidate School, and upon graduation he would receive a commission in the Marine Corps with a guaranteed opportunity to attend flight school. It happened so fast he could not completely understand why he had done it; it was as if some fire he could not turn off took over the minute he saw the poster.

The recruiter warned Samuel, "Watch your eyes; they have to stay perfect the rest of your time in college, and then all you have to do is graduate to be commissioned."

Samuel took that to mean, "Don't study too hard." So he became a math major (not much reading), joined a fraternity, partied, and worked out like a gladiator to prepare for the Marines. Although he would occasionally write a bad poem after a night of drinking, the creative muse of his youth was neglected along with the warning

"You will suffer."

Years later, Samuel sits in a Waffle House restaurant outside Wilford Hall Medical Center, San Antonio, Texas. It is 2:00 in the morning, and Samuel has not slept for over two weeks. Along with the sleepless nights, he has been undergoing physical therapy for his back in the morning followed by afternoon sessions with a psychiatrist for his insomnia and Post

Traumatic Stress Disorder. Tired of staring at the tepid walls of his base officer quarters, he leaves to kill some time, read the paper, and incite his insomnia with a pot of coffee.

"What can I do for ya?" a tired-looking waitress drawls to Samuel. She's been on shift for almost six hours and the Waffle House is empty save for her, Samuel, and the cook.

"Oh," Samuel pauses as he looks up from his paper and scans the menu. "I'll just have some coffee and half an order of biscuits and gravy."

"Be right up." The waitress forces a smile and then walks away.

Samuel picks his paper back up, and then it hits him.

TOOK A STORM

The words pulse in his head and won't let up.

TOOK A STORM TOOK A STORM TOOK A STORM TOOK A STORM TOOK A STORM TOOK A STORM TOOK A STORM TOOK A STORM TOOK A STORM TOOK A STORM TOOK A STORM TOOK A STORM

"Here ya go, hon," the waitress states as she sets down Samuel's coffee. Before she can walk away, Samuel asks her a question.

"Do you have a pen I can borrow?"

"Well, sure, hon," she answers agreeably. "What do ya need it for?"

"Oh nothin'," Samuel shrugs. "Just need to write something down."

"Here ya go." She smiles again and hands Samuel the pen. He immediately grabs a napkin and begins to write, and the words flow.

TOOK A STORM
TO CRACK THE MORTAR
THE STONE
THE ANCIENT CLAY…

In less than five minutes he has written a poem for the first time in four years. For a moment, joy seeps through his body, and he is happy again. Then the feeling fades as he stares out the window into a black night. Familiar demons begin to heckle him, and, consumed with fear, his mind descends into a black hell of guilt, fear, and paranoia.

"Sir, sir, sir!" The waitress almost yells at Samuel.

"Huh?" Samuel looks up.

"Sorry to bother you, sir, but you've been sitting there for over half an hour, staring straight ahead." She puts her hand on Samuel's shoulder. "You haven't touched your food or coffee."

"Uh, oh, I'm sorry," Samuel answers groggily. "Would you mind getting me another cup?"

"Sure," she smiles.

Samuel's head slumps to his hands. He is tired of suffering, and he only sees one answer.

"I'll keep writing and try to make sense of it all," he reassures himself.

That very night, back at the base, he finishes off another poem and sleeps for the first time in two weeks. It is not long, only a couple hours of fitful rest, but it is a welcome start.

SKINNY DIPPIN'

Took a storm

To crack the mortar

The stone, the aged clay

The walls I'd built to shield myself

From rains I feared to face

Took a storm

To clear the rubble

The remnants of my home

To find the lost foundation

Poured before I dwelt alone

And the waters flow

So today

I think I'll swim

"I shall not die, but live…"

Psalm 118:17

STORMS

The Lady of the Lake's hand rises high from the water as I enter a rotting rowboat dying on the lake's shore. Miraculously, it floats, and I begin rowing towards her. Although I can only see her arm, she is hypnotic. The silken skin of her wrist glows soft and delicate, her fingers long, thin, and ageless like an alabaster sculpture. Blowing with the wind in a rhythm of ripples and soft waves, a light blue sleeve adorns her arm.

Rowing feverishly, sweat begins to collect heavy and thick on my brow. I seem to be moving steadily, but I draw no closer to her.

Anxiousness quickens my pace, and the Lady answers my exertion by opening her hand with the grace of a flowing wave. In her palm appears a thick black book. Remarkably, although I still must be twenty yards from her, I can see the lettering on the spine. My name, SAMUEL, is written in bold red letters.

"What is that?" I wonder as I row even faster.

Sweating profusely with every muscle in my body aching, the lure of her hand and my curiosity to examine the book increase my strength – strength that builds as the skies around me darken, and a gale blasts fiercely across the water. Storm clouds invade, sweeping in like enormous ghosts. They blacken the sky and the temperature plummets, causing my skin to sprout enormous goose pimples.

Dimly, masked by the rustling of leaves from the swaying trees surrounding the lake, I hear a faint voice calling me to shore:

"Do not continue. The Lady is death. The Lady is death."

But I can't stop; she must be good and beautiful. And besides, I'm gradually drawing closer. I will reach her.

The storm continues to build. In the forested hills surrounding the lake, whirling tornadoes thoughtlessly tear trees from the earth and then toss them like balsa toothpicks. All of this destruction fills the air with the debris of nature: earth, animals, and anything else in its destructive path.

Mercilessly, the storm increases its fury. Above the lake, funnel clouds reach for the sky in turbulent, aquatic dervishes. Fish struggle to swim from the vertical current carrying them away, but their frantic attempts to dive back into the water are futile. None escape. All are carried away into the dark, swirling whirlpool above.

"Noo...!!" I scream.

Desperate and as exhausted as those fish must feel, the lady seems so far away. I have moved perhaps fifty yards since I began, but that was in calm waters. Till now the storm has steered clear of me, but between myself and the lady is bedlam, and it is a bedlam that I am not quite ready to face. I rest, laying the oak handles in my lap as I bend over to take a few deep breaths.

Before I am able to stop panting, I am jerked to attention by a stiff wind that peppers my face with water spray, stinging my skin like BBs. Energized, I begin to paddle again, determined to reach the lady. I cannot be stopped.

But my confidence is short-lived. Glancing down into the boat, I discover that the rotten wood floor is now leaking. I try to scoop the flood out with my hand, but it is futile. Water is pouring in faster than I can bail. Afraid and confused, I begin to long for the solid ground of shore. It can't be that far away. I am sure of it. Fatefully, I decide to row back, but as I turn the boat around, water pours in even faster. Over the sides and up from the holes in the bottom, water fouls my rickety craft like a relentless demon spitting the whole of the Colorado River.

Desperate for hope, I glance back at the Lady, only to see her arm descending into the water. My name can no longer be seen on the binder, although both the Lady and the book seem much closer than before.

They're only a few feet away!
My god, what have I done?
How, how did I draw so close?

My whole being screams, pleading with me not to return to shore. It wants the lady; it wants the book.

"God, I must have them!" Abruptly, I stop rowing and lunge toward the Lady's hand. She is so close.

As I rise from the boat, a deafening roar forces me to hesitate. It is a furious, metallic crescendo like that of a locomotive. Looking up, I see a funnel of stirring air almost fifty feet wide. I am terrified, but before I can scream it descends upon me, snatching me from the boat like a rag doll. As I'm hurled skyward to meet the storm, I remember anguished words from a cross on Golgotha:

"My God, my God, why hast thou forsaken me?"

I am awake now, covered in sweat, my flannel sheets and pillow soaked through. After sitting up and wiping my face, I walk over to my desk and begin to write, trying to forget the black masked man that torments me, the demon riding on my shoulder.

FLY AWAY

Samuel was a boy, and he wanted to fly. From the edge of his bed, he would stare out his window for hours following the birds and clouds as they painted a portrait of magic against the canvas of a deep blue sky. Dusk was his favorite time to watch, and just before the sun would sink to bed, he would gaze upon its orange glow and dream of soaring, creating a magic of his own.

So one day, Samuel walked out upon his front porch, stepped forward, and grabbed its latticed rail tightly. As determination and fired inspiration built within, he began to sway. Back and forth he went, and as his face became stone hard, his skin etched deeply with furrows of resolve. He had made up his mind.

"I am going to fly."

Like an agile cat he leapt atop the porch's rail, and a warm surge began pulsating through his body. The early spring air pricked his skin, and a slow breeze moving across the neighboring cornfields allowed his long, blond hair to swim. His cheeks glowed like a campfire as they drank in the last warming glares of the sinking sun.

Inside, Samuel was running out of control. A raging fire screamed, "Fly!! I'll only stop if you fly."

Calmly, he glanced at the ground below, then back at the sky; and with the casualness of crossing a quiet street after checking for traffic, he leapt. And then he flew.

Or should I say soared. His arms and legs stretched wide like a parachute, while his face steered straight toward the golden sun. Cooled by the flowing wind, his internal burning settled to a comforting warm throb. But more importantly, with every foot that rushed by, bad memories and despairing feelings trailed away as his soul was cleansed in the exhilaration of flying.

He was free.

Although flying was like floating on pure adrenaline and testosterone, his emotions did slowly settle, and he was able to relax. The wind cooled his face, and the furnace within it burned in defiance of gravity. Floating with clouds, he bathed in the blue sky as his legs and arms hung free. His smile remained, and it was calm, even serene.

As if he was on a lazy Sunday afternoon drive, Samuel casually explored his new playground. Turned over on his back with his hands behind his head, he floated like a tourist in the salty waters of the Dead Sea. Alone in the sky, he began to believe the heavens were his exclusive domain. But before these grandiose thoughts could blossom further, the sound of flapping wings woke Samuel from his daydreaming.

Startled by the culprits that dared to invade his private sanctuary, he began to tumble and spin through the air like a falling cat. When he was finally able to balance himself, he was greeted with majesty. It was nothing that could be found staring across cornfields. A flock of twenty-four bald eagles dotted the sky in a perfectly spaced triangular flight pattern. Their wing tips flapped just inches apart, a model of precision, while they kept their bodies rigid and their heads held high. These knights of the sky soared effortlessly.

Samuel couldn't help but puff out his chest thinking, "Hey, I'm flying with the eagles. But why? Why have they come to me?"

Then in flew the answer. The leader of the pack broke away from the point of the pyramid and flew toward Samuel. He was not only the largest of the eagles, but he also appeared to be the oldest. A touch of gray speckled the feathers of his white head and his eyes seemed wiser, more penetrating than the rest. In no time he was upon Samuel and along with the rest of the pack slowed to a glide; all of their gigantic wings were spread wide and seemed to float on the wind.

The eagle took a minute to size Samuel up, then bowed his head respectfully and began to speak. "My name is Aidan, leader of the Golden Wing eagle pack. We've been following you since the beginning of your flight. It was decided that now would be an appropriate time to approach you." Aidan paused as the other eagles nodded in agreement.

"We mean no harm, but we must have some information. What is your name, and would you please be kind enough to state your business? In case you're wondering why we want to know these things, well, it's simple. It's our business to know these things."

The eagle coldly stared into Samuel's eyes, a glare devoid of any emotion. He wanted answers as direct as his questions had been. Samuel was not nearly as cool. He was shocked. His body shook and his heart raced as he tried to size up the talking bird in front of him. Remarkably, he was able to spit out an answer.

"My, my name is Samuel. I wanted to fly, so I jumped off my porch and here I am."

"That's all?" Aidan exclaimed, unimpressed.

"That's all," Samuel shrugged.

"But where are you going? When are you returning to your perch?" the eagle ask. He looked very confused now.

"I don't even know how I'm flying much less where I am going." Exasperated, Samuel threw his hands up in the air. He had been hoping the eagles had these answers.

"And you are human?"

"Yes, I am human." What a dumb question, Samuel

thought.

"Humans don't fly." The eagle was puzzled. "Isn't that right?"

"Generally speaking," Samuel rolled his eyes and tried his best not to scream. Is this eagle as clueless as I am? he thought.

"This is very unusual," Aidan replied. "We've never seen a human flying before. Let me talk with the council. I'll be back."

As suddenly as he had appeared, Aidan broke away and flew high into the sky about one hundred yards above Samuel and the rest of the eagle pack. He then let out a whistle shrill enough to crack glass, if there had been any around, and immediately four other eagles left the formation and joined him in a circular holding pattern.

Samuel was utterly confused.

What's going on? he wondered. Do these birds have anything to do with my flying? How can they talk?

That was as far as Samuel's questioning got before Aidan returned and the rest of the council rejoined the formation. Once again Aidan stared at Samuel silently. After a moment, he cleared his throat and spoke in a voice even sterner than before.

"You must return, Samuel."

"What?!" Samuel shouted. He became even more muddled and panicked. This proclamation of Aidan's made no sense.

"Return? I can't return. Please help me. I need help," he pleaded.

"You must go back, boy human. This is all far too strange and improper. And look at you. Hah!! What a sight for flying. You shouldn't even be flying. Something, probably evil, must be helping you."

This departure from respectfulness shook Samuel and he wondered, What have I done? Do I threaten them?

21

He answered Aidan with the only truth he knew at the moment. "I, I know it's weird, but that's why I think I can't return. I can't help what I'm doing."

Before Aidan could reply, Samuel began speeding away in a streaking blur. Whatever had brought him here decided it was time for Samuel to leave. Aidan struggled to catch him, but he couldn't keep up. As Aidan faded into the distance, Samuel could hear him yelling. It was a warning the likes of which Samuel had heard before and would hear again.

"You will fall, human! You are not meant to fly. This power will abandon you and you will fall."

Samuel tried to speak, to explain, but at the speed he was flying, whenever he opened his mouth the pounding wind filled it with air, and nothing escaped but silence. Far away he could see Aidan joining the pack. With Aidan in position on point, the eagles flew away from Samuel in a high, looping arc. They were turning their backs on him in a pageantry of flapping wings.

"What am I doing here?" Samuel despaired out loud.

"I don't belong."

FLYING WITH CLIPPED WINGS

Eaten by laughter

Blood drips from their smile

And I stumble on

Stumble on

Samuel continued to fly. Like a sick child waking on Christmas morning to open presents, he soon forgot about the pain and confusion he had just suffered and concentrated on flying.

"I am flying!!" screamed the smile stitched across his face.

Gazing about, Samuel marveled at the endless kaleidoscope stretched wide across the horizon. The clouds flowed long and cottony, absorbing magical combinations of light from the sky like a starving artist. The sun still hung majestically, right where it had been at the beginning of Samuel's flight. It drew Samuel and he rose high into the atmosphere where the vast blackness of space meets the ethereal blue of earthly skies.

Looking out at the stars, he was a contemporary, a fellow resident of heaven. Samuel truly felt free of earthly bondage.

A rare moment indeed.

GOD KILLED AN ANGEL

Why do people dwell in the dark recesses of their minds, allowing self-doubt and depression to invade like mutating viruses? When do they cross over from the ignorant bliss of youth to the regrettable despair of a purposeless adult struggling to exist, waiting to die?

Samuel could not remember. He had passing remembrances of a small boy free in the world, a boy who was currently consumed with escaping it. He did not know from whom or what; it just seemed to him that every bit of unfairness touched his life without concern for his happiness. Most nights he would lie in his bed, stare at the ceiling, and try to dream of places far away from his home. Magic places, fairy places, places where he could be free to run and play and rest.

Other nights were different. This was one of those nights. These nights, Samuel was convinced a twelve-year-old could be insane and not know why. He'd never been molested, never been beaten by his parents, nothing traumatic he could imagine causing this. Nothing that could explain his morbid companionship with a twenty-gauge shotgun – a present on his twelfth birthday.

With the conviction of a penitent monk, Samuel lay on his bed grinding the muzzle of the shotgun deep into his temple. It did not take long for the pain to become dull numbness, and as his skin ripped away, blood dripped down the side of his head, littering the pillow with dark red spots.

As the barrel twisted deeper and deeper towards his skull, he did not flinch. He just stared toward the ceiling with unblinking, bloodshot eyes – eyes that were a looking glass into the soul of a boy who tonight saw death as a sweet release, a kind of justice for the pain that churned inside him.

The cold metal of the shotgun's barrel was becoming a perverse joy. It held a power he longed for, but feared. The power to change life. The power to end his misery.

But pain and suicidal thoughts alone were not enough to satisfy the sickness festering deep in Samuel's calloused heart. He wanted a witness to his torment. It was time for someone to share this torturous vigil.

"Mom, could ya come here, please. I need to talk," Samuel quietly called, coaxing his mother to the stillness of his disheveled room.

"Yeah, one minute, honey. Let me put these biscuits in the oven," she casually replied.

"Sure, Mom, it can wait," Samuel answered.

But could it wait? Morbid despair and apocalyptic dreams consumed him, both forging time into one long breath – a breath he hoped would soon end. A breath he had been holding while his soul burst. A breath he thought only a shotgun could relieve him of.

Little waiting was required, as a few minutes later he heard his mother's approaching footsteps. Her heavy feet echoed down the hallway, and Samuel became overwhelmed with fear and anxiety. After curling his hand tightly around the wooden stock, he fingered the shotgun's trigger. The knuckles of his fist flushed white and veiny.

"What do ya need, Samuel?" She called from the hallway.

Samuel remained silent as he waited for her to enter the room. Just as he could hear her begin to turn the doorknob, she called out to someone else.

"What's that? Oh, no." Then she directed her voice to

Samuel. "Samuel, honey, I'm sorry. Jill Jenkins is at the door. I totally forgot about bridge tonight. I'll talk to you when I get back, honey." But she would forget, and the talk would never happen.

Without waiting for a reply, she ran back down the hallway to greet her visitor. Samuel didn't reply – he just lay motionless on his bed, sweat dripping down the slick tenderness of his youthful skin. His face looked eerily relaxed, but his eyes were as hollow as those of a soulless corpse. Silence and pain settled over the room like a deep, suffocating fog, but one voice managed to penetrate the murkiness of Samuel's mind: "I am crazy."

But he'd wished for that before. Craziness. A way to escape or make sense of his despair. Salvation was never found. But he would not think about that today. Today Samuel was flying.

Samuel followed the roll of the land, skimming over a checkered tapestry of fields and farmhouses. Silos sprang up like pinball machine obstacles, and clouds formed mysterious and heavenly mazes.

It was easy to feel special, even chosen, and right now all he wanted to think about was where he would explore next and what wild maneuvers he would attempt on the way.

With his eyes sharply focused, like those of a hawk seeking game in brush hundreds of yards away, he began a looping turn, high into the limitless ceiling of the blue sky. At the top of the arc, just as he seemed to be losing momentum, he turned toward the ground in a violent twist that quickly resulted in a pulse-pounding, ferocious dive. His glazed look from the night before was now replaced with one of exhilaration, and like a crazed banshee; he screamed, "Yaheeee!!!"

Blazing along like a bullet at terminal velocity, Samuel rapidly lost altitude as he drew closer to earth. Just a moment before impact, he pulled away in a gut-wrenching carnival ride recovery. Missing the top of a pine tree by inches, ecstasy pumped through his body. He had never felt so alive. Every cell tingled. His whole being was one large smile.

Deluded with heavenly grandeur, he began planning for an even wilder maneuver. But much to his surprise, he was interrupted by a small hilltop community that appeared ahead of him.

It was an encampment of brightly colored tents. Simply constructed of green, blue, and yellow canvas, they were scattered haphazardly all along what was a treeless hill. Among the tents were small campfires. Although unattended, they all burned brightly.

The camp was neat, tidy, and free of trash. Nothing seemed out of place or unneeded. Approaching the periphery, he could not see any people. As he drew closer, he noticed the center of the camp was located in a hollow circled by thick brush.

Deep in the hollow raged the largest bonfire Samuel had ever seen. Flames violently licked the air, whipping off the tips of immense logs. "Where did the logs come from?" Samuel wondered. It was a miracle the fire hadn't set the surrounding brush on fire. Even more amazing was what Samuel discovered gathered around this blaze. They were the answer to the foremost thought running through Samuel's mind.

"Who lives here?"

Before a closer investigation of the campers could take place, a fog of pain drifted into Samuel's head and all he could see, hear, or feel was PS 21. That is, James Washington

Elementary School, Public School 21.

Samuel had been a sheltered child brought up in the security of Littleton, a small farm town in rural Indiana. His elementary school was small and comforting. The playground was full of innocent laughter, and the teachers always seemed to be smiling.

There were only about twenty students in Samuel's class, and they were all friends. Daily topics of conversation tended to be about chores, Little League baseball, and who had a crush on whom. Most of the children even brought brown paper bag lunches lovingly packed by their mothers. It was more *Happy Days* and *Brady Bunch* than even Richie Cunningham or Marcia Brady could have imagined. The summer before Samuel's fifth-grade year, though, everything changed. His family moved, and Samuel's world was turned upside down.

Samuel's father was a pastor, so it was expected, but still a shock to young Samuel. His new home was again in the country; a plain abode nestled among a small church, bean and cornfields. But that is where any similarities to life in Littleton ended. The "Littleton" of his new county was a slum, a dying suburb, a town where most of the checks people cashed had welfare written on them. It was one of the state's many forgotten cities, and amidst the barrenness that was Mayfair, Indiana, sat Mayfair Elementary School. To here Samuel was bused – a long bus ride that soon became an endless journey to a teary-eyed abyss, followed later in the day by a return trip that was nothing less than a desperate flight to freedom.

"Sissy preacher's boy. You never kissed a girl, have you, sissy?"

These words and others like them followed Samuel wherever he went. Little League and tractor talk was nonexistent; instead, the children wanted to shoot the bull. They boasted of getting laid like older brothers and sisters and reveled in predicting what "punk" was going to get beaten up that day. Usually it was Samuel.

"You think you are so freaking smart the way ya always answer the teacher's questions. Don't mean nothin', cause you know we can kick your little butt."

But Samuel wasn't little; he only cowered that way. Growing up around farms, his tall frame was muscled for a small boy, and his hands were weathered and hard.

The children circled Samuel at recess in the dusty confines of the school's playground. With nowhere to run and escape their taunts and too afraid to fight back, he usually just sat down. Then he would hide his head between his knees and pray the taunting would go away. That is what his mother told him, anyway — pray.

"Yeah, we're going to whip you, Sammy."

Sitting still and prayer did not seem to work, though, and gradually something began to change inside Samuel. His fear slowly turned to rage, and finally one day he stopped crying.

"Thanks for the lunch money, ya wussy," Ricky Kabacinski bragged as he snatched the dollar sticking out of Samuel's pocket. "I'm gonna buy a Twinkie with this. Thank your mommy for me. Momma's boy."

Samuel had been standing and he did not move when Ricky acted, but something unwound inside his head, and his eyes began to burn in a hellish glare. Young Ricky had never seen anything like it. He felt the fear in Samuel turn to hateful malice and he wanted to run. But the hate in Samuel's eyes paralyzed him.

"I'll kill you! I hate you!" Samuel screamed as he reached

out and grabbed Ricky. Ricky tried to pull away but it was too late. Samuel's large hands were choking him.

Samuel became eerily silent. His eyes opened wide as Ricky's face grew redder, gasping for air. He pulled Ricky to the ground and began to pound his face with both fists. Samuel still said nothing.

"Stop it, Samuel," Ricky wailed between blows, "I'm sorry. Please stop!"

Samuel's reply was short, emotionless.

"Go to hell."

And he kept beating. By the time the teachers came Ricky was a bloody mess, and Samuel no longer cowered. Every child stood staring as Samuel was escorted off the playground. Some of their mouths hung open while others were too afraid to show any reaction at all. None of them spoke, and none of them would ever pick on Samuel again.

But life was larger than Mayfair Elementary School. Wherever Samuel went and felt disrespected, he fought, and as he grew older, more athletic, and popular, he charmed. But charm could not erase fear, and Samuel was chased by fear – fear that brought loneliness.

Alone in a world he wanted so badly to embrace, he walked through life like the little boy in the playground, praying to be seen for what he was inside: gentle, compassionate, a child who liked to pray with his mother.

It made him sick. So he ran away from that little boy. He thought no one knew. But they knew.

ALONE

A hose in my yard

Did not move

As the rain fell

And the grass grew

Taller the blades

Reached for the sky

Breathing rays

That they may not die

And the hose

Lay still

WHO AM I?

Back at the hill Samuel was still alone, hovering above what looked like a merry group of, for lack of a better description, elves. They all were dancing, hand in hand, singing and laughing around the bonfire.

Samuel began to slowly descend. Fear and trepidation swelled within him. His fear proved unfounded, though, as he ventured closer to the group. Neither a word nor glance was given in his direction. He was as unnoticed to the frolicking crowd as still air.

As Samuel settled just a few feet above the festivities, the peculiarity of these people became clear. They were barefoot and outfitted in the oddest collection of apparel he had ever seen. Some wore long-tailed tuxedos; others dressed in the fruity attire of a festive Hawaiian luau. Corduroy, flannel, polyester, purple, aqua, and jade - every material and color known to man seemed to be represented. And they all wore or waved hats of velvet that sprouted long plumes of ostrich feathers from their tips.

They also looked quite jolly, which suited their universally short, plump bodies. In fact, none were taller than four feet, and they all seemed quite capable of rolling on their stomachs like tight little bowling balls. Crossing all their faces were broad smiles that appropriately complemented their rosy cheeks. Samuel grinned and imagined *The Hobbit's* reluctant hero, old Bilbo Baggins – albeit a more bohemian version.

Dancing together around the fire, these joyous vagabonds moved as one. Lovingly they held hands as they danced a playful jig of hopping feet and bobbing heads. Accompanying this festive dance, they sang. Over and over they repeated the same brotherly tune, and Samuel soon found himself singing along.

Come, friend, round bright fire

We sing of heart's desire
Our fears together belay

Sweet dreams all together
Through sunny
Or stormy dark weather
Dear friends, our journey the same
We'll feel so completely
Heartfelt sung sweetly,
Come friend
And join in our games

In the end all together
We will surely agree,
Dark fears, no hope?
What a shame

From joy they'll derail you
Never let them prevail you
Grab your friends
And teach them the same

Samuel, hypnotized by this joyful melody of brotherhood, felt drawn to the melancholy below. As he drew near, one of the elves stepped out of the circle. Then with no warning, this same elf looked up, reached out, and plucked him out of the air.

Samuel was again on firm ground. He stood facing the elf that had snatched him, and what a strange-looking little fellow he discovered him to be. Easily a foot or more shorter than Samuel, he wore scuffed red and white shoes that Samuel quickly recognized were identical to a pair he had rented once at Lucky's

Bowling Alley in Littleton. Tightly adorning the elf's plump
body was a plaid suit, worn and wrinkled, that loosely held a
corncob pipe from one of its torn pockets. The tiny man's skin
was bright pink and his hair was a long, tangled, white mess that
dangled off his shoulders and down his back.

As harmless and funny as the elf looked, Samuel still
became frightened as the lucidness and reality of the situation
collided with what had been a dreamy journey. He wanted to
speak, but his lips were curled tightly, unable to move, and
lumps rather than words gathered in his throat. The elf had no
such fearful hesitation.

He tugged on Samuel's sleeve and asked, "Please, my
friend, come join us. Put away that fearful expression and enter
our merry circle. You will soon be one of us. Jolly. Dancing.
Happy!"

"Yee hee!" The other elves giggled with glee at the
prospect of a new companion. They all called out in a hopeful
chorus, "Come, friend, come join us. Share in our song. You
will forget your troubles, because here is where you belong. Hee
hee!"

Samuel felt overwhelmed, but the lumps disappeared, and
he was able to ask what seemed the most natural of questions.

"What is your name?"

But this puzzled the elf.

"What do you mean, 'name'?" he asked.

"I mean, what do you call yourself? I'm called Samuel. I
have friends named Ryan, Casey, and Mark."

"Hmm, very interesting." The elf stroked his stubbly chin.
"Well, we don't have those. Very impractical, you see. We're one
group, one family. You'll just have to give up that nonsense."

Samuel was equally puzzled at the elf's reply, but oddly

the prospect of losing his name and joining the group seemed inviting, and certainly easy. They were so eager for him to join.

Their song echoed in his head.

"Come, friend, round bright fire, we sing 'bout heart's desire..."

That was enough to make up his mind. Samuel had never felt so unconditionally accepted by a group like this in his life, and the elves were so genuinely friendly.

So what if I give up my name, he thought. This life seems so easy.

"Yes, I will join you," Samuel smiled, proud of his decision. The plaid elf was just as happy.

"Wonderful, wonderful. Step forward and we will continue the festivities. Everybody, begin!"

The singing continued but as Samuel stepped forward to join them – whoooooosh!!!

He felt a jerk and was sent soaring from the camp. The friendly hilltop soon became a distant speck. Desperate to return, he struggled wildly, grasping and clawing toward the village. But away he flew.

The sun had fallen further below the horizon, and air that had been invigorating was now piercingly cold. The shooting wind bit deep into Samuel's skin. He surrendered to the frigid assault and began to clench his shivering body. No relief came. His panicked mind raced for answers when, bamm!!

The sky spit him out.

Samuel screamed as he began to fall, quickly losing touch with sanity. His mind began a meltdown.

"Stop! Ahh!!" he pleaded as he fell faster and faster. He expected to die; in fact, he would feel this way again.

One of Samuel's dreams as a small boy had been to

become a jet pilot, a fighter ace. Fate would grant his wish.

Years later, a grown man of twenty-five harnessed the power of a jet aircraft, and the boy inside gleamed proudly. Like a bold eagle Samuel soared through the sky, his jet a supersonic oasis of triumph and pride.

"If only those kids could see me now. I'm the man!" he would boast to himself while fleeing from old feelings he had never been able to overcome.

The problem was that deep inside he didn't believe it. He had never stopped running from the voices that told him he would fail. He was at the mountaintop and all he could do was fear falling down. And fall down he did.

FLAMETHROWER

Age 25

Oceana Naval Air Station

Oceana, Virginia

"Look at that sucker fly," Samuel boasted as his drive landed in the fairway three hundred yards away. Lieutenant Dave Skinner shook his head as they both headed for their golf cart. They were on the sixth hole of the Oceana Naval Air Station golf course and were trying to get in a round, although the sky looked as if it could burst open with thunder, lightning, and rain at any minute. Their scheduled flight for the day had been canceled, and they wouldn't be leaving Oceana for their home base in Meridian, Mississippi, until the weather cleared.

"You got more luck than a one-eyed mute in a whorehouse!" Lieutenant Skinner laughed as they drove off toward their balls.

"Ain't luck, I just hit 'em like angels!" Samuel replied.

Lieutenant Skinner chided, "Heaven – good God, you got a heaven anecdote for any occasion."

"Guess I'm getting under your atheist's thick skin," Samuel smiled good-naturedly. He and Lieutenant Skinner had spent most of the morning debating religion. It was clear Lieutenant Skinner was a "devout" atheist who looked down upon anyone ignorant enough to put their faith in a sick myth.

"Don't forget who's got rank," Lieutenant Skinner wryly smiled. "It's bad enough I gotta fly with someone who puts faith in make-believe. You're likely to do something stupid."

Samuel grinned and retorted, "Well, if we do something stupid at least I know where I'll be going!"

Lieutenant Skinner didn't answer immediately. They had

just reached their balls in the fairway, and he jumped out of his cart to position himself for his next swing.

"I tell you what, Samuel," Lieutenant Skinner smiled. "I'll hit this one for Jesus himself." He addressed the ball, then after a pause, Lieutenant Skinner swung, and the ball sailed toward the green where it landed within inches of the hole.

The following morning, a dreary Saturday, Lieutenant Skinner was anxious to leave and woke up Samuel early to prepare for their flight. His wife was eager for him to return, and he was tired of being on the road. So even though storm clouds covered the sky and rain was falling, he wasn't about to spend another day in Oceana. As they walked toward the ready room in the rain, he consoled Samuel.

"Don't worry, kid; I've flown in soup like this a thousand times."

"But this is an instrument flight, and I'm supposed to be under the training bag, taking off blind. What if something goes wrong in this weather?" Samuel questioned.

"C'mon, I'll be up front looking out for us, and if anything goes wrong I'll take control." Skinner patted Samuel on the back.

Even though the tower said it wasn't safe to take off with a training flight in these conditions, Skinner took advantage of a short break in the weather to rush a takeoff.

"Samuel, don't worry about your preflight check. Just go out to the plane, call tower for takeoff clearance, and get ready." He paused as Samuel looked incredulous and then continued, "I'll file the flight plan and we'll get out of here before the weather gets bad again."

"But I can't do that. I could get grounded for not doing a

flight check," Samuel stated pleadingly.

"Kid, we're not at our home base, so nobody is going to care. Now get your ass in the plane, and I'll take care of everything," Skinner ordered as he pushed Samuel toward the aging T-2 Buckeye waiting on the tarmac.

Samuel shuffled toward the plane, increasingly nervous about a flight that was being rushed, and being rushed is something an inexperienced flight student finds disorienting. He gave the plane a quick glance but was afraid to perform a flight check and incur Skinner's wrath.

After fastening his ejection harness, he settled into the cockpit and began to check his flight instruments. Before he could finish his checklist he heard Lieutenant Skinner on his intercom. He looked up to see Lieutenant Skinner in the seat in front of him strapping in.

"You ready?"

"Well, sure, but that was fast. Did you complete preflighting the plane?" Samuel's voice cracked.

"Thoroughly," he lied. The plane had been preflighted earlier in the morning, but that flight was scrapped because of the weather, so Skinner let that be a good excuse for not checking it now. Of course, that meant he hadn't looked in the electrical compartment. And that meant he would not find the fraying wire that had recently burnt through and would soon cause a short circuit or worse.

"Ah, all right," Samuel stammered.

Vroom! Skinner started the jet and spoke to Samuel over the intercom.

"Whad'ya say, Samuel? Ready to go fly?" Lieutenant Skinner spoke through the Intercockpit Communication System (ICS) of the McDonnell-Douglas T-2 Buckeye, the United States

Navy and Marine Corps jet trainer.

"Yeah, sure, but now my instruments are checking out weird. The heading indicator keeps drifting, and the attitude gyro is fluttering up and down."

As Samuel replied, he tapped the glass face of the heading indicator, futilely hoping it would stop its abnormal antics. The Buckeye had been in the Navy's inventory for over thirty years, and glitches like this were a familiar and bothersome occurrence.

"Samuel," Lieutenant Skinner continued, "if we write it up, we won't have time to grab another jet today. Look at the weather. Those clouds are moving in fast."

Samuel was getting nervous, but ultimately he wanted Lieutenant Skinner, his instructor, to think he was a gung ho student.

"You are right. I need this instrument check ride. If we don't get it out today, I might have to do it back in Meridian. You know that can be a bitch. Let's give it a try."

"All right then, I'll back you up on my instruments. Call me if anything gets worse."

"Roger that," Samuel replied.

Skinner then lowered their Plexiglas canopy and began to taxi the Buckeye towards the departure end of the runway.

Samuel was in the Buckeye's rear cockpit. On this particular flight, he would be practicing his instrument flying. The training was intensified by a bag that was snapped into place on a section of canopy above and around Samuel. This ensured that Samuel was blind to anything outside his own cockpit. In this way, he could only use the cockpit's instruments to orient himself.

Skinner was sitting in the front cockpit. He was along to critique Samuel's performance, taxi the jet on the ground, and, of course, supply a set of eyeballs to the world outside.

"Samuel, I'll go ahead and call for takeoff. At eighty knots the jet is yours. Keep it straight, referencing your heading indicator. I'll be watching in case it acts up."

"Roger, sir," Samuel replied. He had taken off blind like this before, but the weather and sloppiness of the preflight made him nervous. Ultimately, though, he was confident in his ability to fly off of instruments, and he had faith that Lieutenant Skinner would see anything unusual and act accordingly.

Approaching the hold-short line, Lieutenant Skinner depressed the radio send switch on the joystick and called for clearance to take off. The Buckeye rested near the departure end of the runway. The hold-short line could not be crossed unless they had clearance from the tower.

"Tower, Navy 3A, ready for takeoff. Number One at the hold-short," Lieutenant Skinner called.

"Navy 3A," tower replied, "you are cleared for takeoff, switch to departure frequency."

"Navy 3A is cleared and switching," Lieutenant Skinner acknowledged the tower.

With that authorization, Lieutenant Skinner taxied onto the runway, switched the radio channels, and called back to Samuel, "You ready to rock?"

"Ready," was Samuel's short reply.

Obediently, Lieutenant Skinner positioned the Buckeye straight down the runway. After pressing his feet up against the brakes to keep the plane still, he ran the engines up to full throttle for a systems check. As the engines roared and the frame of the Buckeye vibrated from the harnessed power, Samuel checked his control stick's freedom of movement and quickly scanned his instruments looking for any abnormalities. He assumed Lieutenant Skinner did the same. Assumed, that is, because as the brakes were released and the jet was sent hurtling down the runway, Samuel failed to hear Lieutenant Skinner's confirmation of his final check over the ICS. Samuel shrugged it off, figuring Lieutenant Skinner was in a hurry and had just forgotten.

"I'll have the jet soon anyway," he falsely assured himself.

He knew he was disobeying the standard operating procedure of the squadron. If he didn't hear Lieutenant Skinner's confirmation of the checks, he should abort. But he continued on.

As the jet approached a hundred knots, Samuel expected to hear the standard three-way change of control call. It was to ensure that any time the jet changed hands, it was clear who was in control. Samuel had been briefed by Lieutenant Skinner that he would take the jet at this point, and he expected the call. It should have sounded like this – short and professional:

"You got the jet."

"Roger, I have controls."

"Roger, you have the controls."

But the exchange did not take place. Samuel heard nothing. He tried to reach Lieutenant Skinner over the microphone, but all he heard was silence. Little did he and Lieutenant Skinner know that at this moment the fraying wire had caused a short circuit, disabling the ICS.

The bag blocked Samuel's vision into Lieutenant Skinner's cockpit. He had no way of knowing what might be wrong with Lieutenant Skinner, and if something was wrong, what was causing it. The jet was passing rotation speed and Samuel needed to make a decision. Did he take control of the plane or wait and see if Lieutenant Skinner acted?

His training told him that he couldn't wait. He would

have to assume something was wrong with Lieutenant Skinner. Because he couldn't see to stop the plane on the runway and there was not enough time to remove the instrument hood, his only choice was to take off.

"It'll be all right," he hoped.

Not quite sure of his decision, Samuel grabbed the control stick and flew the Buckeye off the runway. Airborne, he tried the mic again. Again there was complete silence.

But now Samuel was in his element. He felt safe and relaxed knowing that once he raised the jet's gear and flaps he would have time to unsnap the hood and check on Lieutenant Skinner. He could then return to the air station if needed.

At an altitude of about a hundred feet and airspeed of well over one hundred knots, Samuel raised the gear. Next, he waited for the T-2 to reach an altitude of three hundred feet and airspeed of 130 knots. This was the altitude and airspeed required to safely raise the flaps.

His hand moved towards the flap lever in anticipation, but strangely the jet seemed to lose acceleration. It was as if the Buckeye had suddenly bogged down in molasses.

"That's strange," he thought to himself.

His instincts were further confirmed by the seat of his pants, which told him that the Buckeye was losing what little altitude it had gained since taking off.

"Losing altitude – my God! We just took off!!" The thought echoed violently, banging off the inside of his skull.

"Lieutenant Skinner!!" Samuel screamed. But he knew there would be no answer. The microphone was dead.

"Lieutenant, Lieutenant Skinner!!" He screamed again. He should have ejected. This low to the ground he could do nothing else, but again he hesitated.

What would they say back at the base? Samuel thought. I can't lose this jet.

Self-talk clouded what should have been a quick, lifesaving decision. He should pull the ejection handle. Instead, he slammed his left hand into the jet's throttle, but it was already fully forward, and all he succeeded in doing was bending the steel shaft of the stick. He should have ejected and sent himself and Lieutenant Skinner to safety. He should act now.

As the aircraft continued to slow and settle, Samuel's scan of the plane's instruments became crazed, and he was unable to read anything. His mind only saw disorder and a confused collection of numbers and dials.

"Lieutenant Skinner!!" He yelled again, but Lieutenant Skinner wasn't going to answer, and there was no one left to help Samuel.

Tumbling over the edge of sanity, his paralyzed mind finally discovered the reason for his dilemma. It was a calamity he feared to consider, but knew in his heart was probably true.

Every hazard light on the instrument panel began to flash, and the warning buzzer blared. Red and yellow lights blinked frantically. Only one thing could cause this much mayhem – fire!

And to make matters worse, soon after the lights went crazy, Samuel glanced at his altimeter. It read ZERO – he was either dead and having an out-of-body experience, or they were within the altimeter's margin of error and about to impact the ground. The fire was in his engines. Samuel's gut and the seat of his pants had been correct; the Buckeye had indeed been robbed of its precious thrust.

"What have I been doing?!" Samuel screamed to himself. "What the hell have I been doing?!"

Thirty feet above the ground and under a bag, blind to

the world, lights flashing, nothing but silence in his headphone, Samuel had never been so alone and frightened in his entire life.

Nearly five seconds after the plane's initial deceleration, trained, conditioned reflexes that should have acted sooner finally took over.

Someone pulled the ejection handle and bammm!! But Samuel's memory had stopped moments before, and he would never remember if he had pulled the handle or not – if he had saved himself, or had been saved by a man who would soon be dead. This question would haunt him.

The ejection seat sent Samuel screaming from the dying Buckeye. But just before ejection, the T-2 had rolled over on its left side; and as a result, Samuel was shot away from the jet, parallel to and merely twenty feet above the ground below. A modern ejection seat would have corrected Samuel's trajectory and sent him skyward, but the old rocket he was riding only went where it was pointed. And that was a problem. He was headed for a grove of trees. If his parachute didn't open soon, he would die.

Seven-tenths of a second behind Samuel, it was Lieutenant Skinner's turn to blast off. (His ejection was an automatic response of the ejection sequence. This time delay ensured the seats would not eject simultaneously and hit each other.)

About the time Lieutenant Skinner left the Buckeye, a sensor in Samuel's parachute pack registered the low altitude and immediately ignited a charge which then blew open the parachute. But by now, Samuel was only a few feet off the ground, still traveling over a hundred miles an hour, and the trunk of large oak tree was only a few yards away. According to all parameters, the parachute shouldn't be able to fully deploy in time, and Samuel should die. He was outside the envelope of survivability. But then Samuel felt a jerk as if the canopy had fully deployed, and a split second later he hit the ground. But what had really pulled him safely from the sky? From the tower and from the quickly approaching emergency vehicle, it appeared as if Samuel's chute had not fully deployed.

Just before he hit the ground, Samuel had seen Lieutenant Skinner go flying by. But his chute didn't open in time, and Lieutenant Skinner's last flight was stopped by a line of trees and brush not ten yards from the end of Samuel's parachute ride. What a few seconds earlier had been a human being was now broken and dying.

Samuel woke fifteen minutes later in an ambulance with no clue how he had arrived there. His feet, head, and hands were strapped to a backboard; his flight suit and restraint harness had been cut down the middle.

As his eyes darted around the ambulance, he struggled to remember anything from the last few minutes of his life. Who had found him? Why did his back hurt so badly? Where was Lieutenant Skinner?

Because of the backboard, he thought for a moment that he might be paralyzed, but he was quickly put at ease after finding he could move his fingers and toes. But then he remembered whacking his face on something during the ejection.

"Hey, man, how's my face look, is it cut up?" Samuel asked the paramedic sitting next to him.

"What's that, sir?"

"My face – how's it look?"

"Fine, sir, you got some bruises but nothing serious. You're gonna be fine."

"How's Lieutenant Skinner?" Samuel queried.

"You mean the other pilot?"

"Yeah, the other pilot, what happened to him?"

"Well, they still hadn't found him when we left. Don't worry about that now, we'll be at the hospital soon."

Tired of speaking, Samuel shut his eyes and tried to remember anything from the last hour of his life, but all he could picture was fire and a dizzying array of warning lights. Soon lulled into a trance by road noise and the drone of the ambulance's exhaust, Samuel's only connection with reality became the throbbing pain in his back.

"We're here, sir."

"Huh?"

"We're at the hospital."

Samuel opened his eyes and thought, Great, just freaking great.

"Where does it hurt, Lieutenant?" a young doctor questioned as he prodded Samuel's stomach.

"My back. I'm sore all over, but the only place it really hurts is my back."

"Sure you aren't tender where I'm poking around?"

"I'm sure," Samuel fumed, "just my back, like I told you before."

The doctors wouldn't tell him anything about Lieutenant Skinner, and no one seemed to believe his back was the only place he hurt badly.

"Well, we're going to have some X-rays taken in a minute," the doctor explained, "but first we want to check you for internal bleeding."

"Internal bleeding? What are you talking about?" The implication of the doctor's statement was a bit ominous for Samuel's comfort.

"We think you're fine, Samuel, but you had to have hit

the ground hard. Something bleeding internally could be very serious. Try to urinate if you can in this collection cup. I'll hold it for you."

Samuel strained, but it only aggravated his back. More aggravating, though, was that he couldn't even tell he had a penis. It was completely numb.

"Sorry, doc, can't get nothing to happen."

"Well, I'll send a nurse to put in a catheter. We have to see if there's blood in your urine."

Shock pasted itself across Samuel's face. In college he had taken a good friend of his, Madison, to the emergency room with a ruptured appendix. After the operation, Samuel had been standing outside the recovery room while a nurse performed a catheterization. Madison – six foot two and two hundred rock-solid pounds – screamed like a baby.

A few minutes later and still thinking about Madison's anguish, a nurse entered holding a long thin tube and a jar of lubricant. Samuel's urge to urinate became desperation, but fear was not going to motivate his bladder. After lubing up the catheter, the nurse grabbed Samuel's penis and began to insert the catheter into his urethra.

"Ah, get it in, get it in!" Samuel begged, trying his best not to squirm and irritate his penis even more.

"One second, sir. Okay, there it is; it's in."

Although the worst was over, if Samuel so much as breathed he could feel the tube scratching inside him.

"Nurse, how long do I have to keep this in?"

"I'll be back in a few minutes. As soon as we get enough fluid we'll take it out." As she turned to leave, an officer from Samuel's squadron entered.

"Hello, ma'am, I'm Captain Anderson from Samuel's

squadron. I need to speak with Samuel for a minute. The doctor said it'd be all right."

"Sure, you go ahead. I'm leaving anyway; I'll be back in a few minutes."

As the nurse walked off Captain Anderson turned to Samuel and said, "How you doing, Samuel?"

"I'm all right, sir, my back hurts, but I think I'll be okay. How's Lieutenant Skinner?"

Captain Anderson's eyes began to water. After looking up at the ceiling for a moment, he wiped away his tears, grabbed Samuel's right arm and then answered him.

"He's dead, Samuel."

Samuel was silent. His face didn't so much as twitch; he just stared at the whitewashed ceiling above him.

No longer processing clear thoughts, the only sound in Samuel's head was static.

"What happened up there, son? One minute you guys are airborne, and the next flames are coming out of your engines." Captain Anderson leaned over him now. The answer to his questions was lying in front of him, but Samuel couldn't help him. He just continued staring, saying nothing.

"Samuel, listen to me." There was tired frustration in Captain Anderson's voice now. "What happened? What caused the fire? Why did you all wait so long to eject?"

Samuel had no answers for the same questions that he had been torturing himself with. Slowly, he turned his head toward Captain Anderson, blinked his eyes a few times, and began to cry. A single tear rolled down his cheek onto his pillow.

"I know it's hard," Captain Anderson said sympathetically, "but we need to know what happened. I'll come back later. Now you get some rest and try to remember anything you can. And

one last thing – your parachute, nobody saw it open in time
to give you a swing and break your fall. How the hell did you
survive?"

"It never fully deployed?" Samuel almost whispered. "But
I felt something jerk me and then I was on the ground. It had to
be the parachute."

"You got me," Captain Anderson rubbed his head, "but
nobody saw that chute fully deploy. You're a miracle, kid."
Captain Anderson patted Samuel on the shoulder and before
turning to leave said, "I'll come back later, and maybe you can
remember more of what happened."

But he didn't want to remember. He just wanted to bury
his pain.

I WAS WONDERING

From one grave to another
One bound in dirt while the other
Wakes to face his every day

How different is death
From my long dreary breath
Can a corpse ever see itself crying

Waking to Hell

I'm standing in a broad field of knee-high grass that extends to the horizon in every direction; but that's all there is – swaying grass, a clear sky, and me. Eager to explore, I begin walking through the field, happy to be clueless about where I'm heading. Still, I'm a bit unnerved – each stride through the waist-high carpet is an awkward and blind one, but after about fifty yards without stepping on or in anything, I'm able to relax and walk naturally.

Well, not quite naturally. You see, my soul seems to have unbound itself from my body: a body that has become a vessel, a vehicle to carry me through this fairyland, a hollow chariot that doesn't burden me.

That's why my steps were so strange. I didn't really feel them; but now that I've grown used to them, I've never felt so sure of myself. Where can't I go like this, what can't I do?

I think I'll walk all the way to the horizon and see if a rainbow waits for me; but maybe not.

"He, he, ha."

The laughter of a small child interrupts my wistful dreaming and what had been a crystal clear sky darkens. I begin to feel my weight, and I'm tired, out of breath, human; but from somewhere, I find the strength to begin running towards the voice.

But do I really want to find him? Do I really want to know why he is here?

"Hee, hoo."

"Uh!" I grunt in alarm, then stumble.

Lost in questions, I seem to stumble over the laughter, but

I still can't see the child. Without waiting to catch my breath, I reach down into the gras, but I don't get far. A voice booms across the plain.

"You'll die tonight, Samuel."

What the hell? That sounds like Lieutenant Skinner. His voice is everywhere but he's nowhere to be seen.

"Ubba, ah, ha," the child gurgles again, and after shaking my head, I resume my search.

"You'll die tonight, Samuel!"

"Ahh! Shut up, stop it!"

Looking up again, the sky has lightened a bit and I'm able to see clearly. But I still can't tell who or what is talking to me, and once more I reach down for the child.

"Not so fast, Samuel."

Before I can look up, I'm pulled by the back of my shirt and jerked into a chair. Leather straps circle my feet and wrists, and a metal band wraps around my head. My captor is an enormous, solid oak electric chair.

"You'll die tonight."

"Shut up, just shut up!" But what good will my screaming do? Storms - I can't escape them.

"You'll die tonight!"

"Ahhhh!!" A crack of lightning jerks me to attention, and I look up to see that the sky has become a swirling cauldron of lightning strikes and leaping plumes of fire. As the storm turns it descends and grows darker until finally the only light is from dancing flames and lightning flashes. This hellish mobile turns my vision into nothing but fuzzy shadows and streaks of blinding light.

"Did you forget something, Samuel?"

"Huh?"

Noticing a small tug on my knee, I glance down, and at my feet is a blond-haired, blue-eyed boy. He seems to be about two, and by the mildly distorted, distant look on his face, a victim of Down's syndrome. It appears my search is over.

Wearing a thin grin he begins to climb into my lap. Struggling to stand up, he giggles and coos, completely unaware that he's in the middle of a storm. But Lieutenant Skinner knows and he won't let me forget.

"You'll die tonight, Samuel."

"Why are you doing this?" I can't understand this mess. It's sick, and why the boy?

"You killed me. What's the mystery, you fool?"

No! I can't believe this. The child's hugging me, laughing into my ear.

"I didn't kill you! It was the plane, it wasn't my fault."

"No, you killed me. You waited too long to pull the ejection handle and you killed me. Maybe you wanted me dead; maybe you didn't want me alive to tell them how you panicked."

"No, no, that's not true! It's not my fault! It's not my fault!"

But he wasn't listening to me. Maybe it WAS my fault. God, I did panic. I did kill him!

"Ahhhhh!"

Lightning strikes nearby, followed by spitting fire that sets the grass around me ablaze. The firestorm is only a few feet above me now, ready to swallow the child and me.

Maybe I deserve this, but why the boy?

Christ, there's a boy in my lap!

He can't do this. He can't be doing this.

"Lieutenant Skinner, no! Not the boy! Not the boy!"

"Ha! Ha! Ha! Bye, Samuel," he answers with a laugh.

I feel a metal post stick up between my legs; it's an ejection handle.

"Bye, Samuel. Keep burning. We'll meet again!"

Then my straps fall away, and trained reflexes pull the handle. But nothing happens, no flight to safety, and the storm settles upon us.

Still holding the ejection handle with my left hand, the other cradles the cooing child while I close my eyes and pray for mercy.

Exhausted and drenched in sweat, Samuel awakens in his hospital bed. It is almost 4:00 a.m., and the hospital is quiet, with only the occasional nurse on rounds disturbing the silence. Staring out his window waiting for the sun to rise, Samuel begins longing for his shotgun and the sick comfort of its cold steel for the first time since childhood.

"What else can deliver me?' he asks himself.

Samuel's only glimmer of hope is the belief that this hell can't get any worse. But it can. And it does.

HOW LONG IS .3 OF A SECOND?

Glancing down to change radio stations

You hear a thump from the child

That just ran in front of your car

Now start counting, and don't stop

Until you've forgiven yourself

ONE WEEK AFTER LIEUTENANT SKINNER'S DEATH

Home outside Meridian, Mississippi

Samuel was lying on a green leather couch as he stared out the window of his living room, where he had been looking upon the glassy surface of Lake Dixie Springs for almost three hours. He would have rather been sitting on the dock below his house fishing or just wasting time, but practically speaking, he was immobilized. A brace covered his body from just above his groin to slightly below his armpits. Slow and achingly painful just to get up and down, it was much easier to stay put.

It didn't take long for the couch to become a cushioned cell. Closing his eyes, he would dream of days before the accident, but the moment he woke any peaceful feelings would immediately vanish. They were always replaced with the realization that he was too sore to rise from bed and too depressed and lazy to do anything anyway. Self-pity had hung a shingle over his home, and Samuel obediently checked in. The Hotel Samuel had become a prison.

"You're lucky it wasn't worse. I'm hopeful you'll fly again," the doctor had told him.

"I'm a pilot. I'll fly again." He tried every day to reassure himself. "Somehow I'll fly again." He needed to be a pilot. He needed that title to avoid being honest with himself, afraid of the truth, because the truth said he was a fraud. A fraud that felt almost thankful for the accident – thankful that he could stop living a lie.

He did not really want to be a pilot anymore. He had felt this way for almost a year, yet he trudged on. Sure, he liked flying most of the time, but the Marines Corps was a world

Samuel had grown to question. It said, Conform and we will take care of you; conform or we will crush you. And worse, the complacency of a peacetime armed forces can lead to an emphasis on style over substance, where the most spit-shined soldier is seen as the best.

Samuel wanted to believe he could fit in and feel safe and accepted. In reality, the little boy was tired of being a military man. He only acted that way because he did not have enough courage to admit it.

After all, he had hidden behind labels for so long it was easy to fool people. The Marine Corps was no exception. To them Samuel was tall, fit, and capable of flying jet aircraft. "Of course, he is one of us," they believed. But he wasn't, and he knew it. Sadly, that didn't matter. He had forgotten what he was behind the labels he wore, and he was too afraid to peel them away and find out.

He needed to be a pilot. But the brace screamed, "NO!! You will not be a pilot again."

It was joined in its rebuke by the mountain of guilt he carried for Lieutenant Skinner's death.

"Lieutenant Skinner is dead. What about me?" Samuel would torture himself.

"Well, I fractured my spine and shrunk a little. Big freaking deal.

"Lieutenant Skinner's rotting flesh is looking up at the inside of a coffin.

"It is my fault he is dead.

"I'm such a fake.

"I should be the one being eaten by worms."

Thoughts like these taunted the lonely confines of Samuel's despondent mind. Dark thoughts, morbid preoccupations that had weaved similar self-defeating webs since childhood.

They had even found their way into Samuel's fragile marriage. It took place after a quick flight to Las Vegas followed by a limousine ride to the Little White Wedding Chapel. Both flights of fancy were fueled by a fear Samuel had carried since childhood. It was a fear that made it hard to find a place where he could stand firm. Indeed, he never found that place. Instead, he ran away from failure and disappointment. His marriage was just another ill-fated escape.

That is what Samuel always seemed to do – escape. He did what it took to get by, to see another day, buoyed along with the hope of someday becoming a "somebody," a fighter pilot. He always looked for the easiest way to do just well enough; it made him an expert at fooling people. Whether it was talking like a man of great achievement or appearing to be contented and carefree, he was lucky and smart enough to mask his laziness. It got him through high school, college, even the Marines, and he began to think he could live life this way forever.

Samuel didn't know it at the time, but when he met Miss Kendra O'Leary he would soon reap the rewards of a blissless life. It was easy to fool himself about Kendra at first. She was an easy girl to please and more than eager to fall in love, just another lonely soul looking for a place to escape to like Samuel. What he didn't know at the time was that there is no such thing as escaping in relationships.

He met Kendra outside a bar in Pensacola, Florida, the cradle of naval aviation. She was a waitress, tall, with a model's body, a come-hither face, and a wardrobe that looked painted on from more than ten feet. Before Samuel knew what was happening, they were caught up in a merry-go-round of sex, volatile breakup, reconciliation, then more sex. Samuel – who had slept with only one other woman in his life, and she had broken his heart – soon felt trapped by the affair. He did not love this girl, but his conscience repeated words his mother had said a thousand times: "You only sleep with the person you are going to marry, Samuel."

Embarrassed to confide in his mother and family about what was going on, he packed his guilt and girl on a plane and headed for Nevada.

The evening of the wedding, they fought at dinner and ended the day sleeping apart. Everything since had been one argument followed by another. Eventually Kendra left him, only to return a day, a week, a month later. It usually depended on how long it took her to tire of partying. Occasionally, it was guilt.

Samuel should have ended the marriage soon after the bungled beginning, but he was too proud to admit he had made a mistake and too full of guilt to tell his wife the truth.

"I didn't want to marry you; I was just too ashamed of myself to do anything else."

As a result, they both suffered; and when the day came that he needed a companion, lover, and best friend more than any time in his life, the only thing he received was venom from a bitter heart.

THAT AIN'T LOVE

Samuel was still staring out his window when he heard the sound of Kendra's car coming up the driveway. She stopped in front of the house, and when the front door slammed, a familiar anxious heat began to swell in his belly.

"Hey!" Kendra called from the kitchen, her greeting cut short by a thirsty swig of Michelob that she had grabbed from the fridge.

"What did ya do today?" Samuel called.

"Work, then Kim and I went out for some drinks. How 'bout you?"

"Not much, sat here on the couch and watched TV," Samuel knew she wouldn't like hearing this one bit.

"You mean you didn't get up?" she asked, taking a long pull of beer.

"No, my back still kills me and I don't like taking all that Percocet. It freaks me out." He could feel an argument brewing.

"Well, the doctor said you could get around if you wanted. You're crazy about the Percocet. I'd be getting high off that." She followed the revealing comment about Samuel's painkiller with another swig of beer and then sat down in an old recliner across the room from him.

"I bet you would," he replied. "Leave me alone. I crushed my lumbar a week ago and shrunk a quarter of an inch. I am in pain. Who gives a crap about some dirty dishes and TV?"

Samuel tried to sit up. But with no painkilling drugs in his tender body, he wasn't able to pull himself up. Kendra took a minute to think about Samuel's statement. Then she blasted him.

"It's not your back. You're just lazy and full of excuses. You're no jet pilot. You're not even a good husband. You just like to bang me."

This was the last thing Samuel wanted or needed to hear. He looked at Kendra and wanted to cry out.

"What have I done to deserve this!?!"

"Help me!!"

"I need someone to help me!!"

Instead, he fired another hurtful round back at her.

"Bang you? Are you kidding? What would you be doing without me – waitressing, whoring around town? If I meet one more pilot that had a wild night of sex with you, I am going to freak out." Along with the word "freak" came a little exasperated spittle from Samuel's lips.

The confrontation continued, accusations and vindictive replies by a couple of old pros. Finally, Samuel gave up, tired of arguing, his back throbbing. A familiar look in his wife's eye had also returned. She'd soon be out drinking, unlikely to be seen for at least a few days. Samuel decided to end the conversation with a whimper. He was tired of fighting.

"Fine, you're right; I'm lazy. Haven't done a worthwhile thing in my life." Samuel was still filled with thick cynicism, but he was slowing down.

"That's right, you're lazy," Kendra followed, "and don't keep lying there like some self-righteous hero. You did nothing heroic. Look at me." She moved from the recliner over to Samuel and lowered her face to within inches of his.

"You are no hero. YOU ARE NOTHING MORE THAN A LOSER, A BIG FRAUD."

Samuel thought of Lieutenant Skinner, the burning plane, the helplessness, the cold, dim light reflecting off the white surroundings of the emergency room.

His reply was a teary-eyed stare through Kendra into the black night. She gave him a second to respond, then stormed off to the bedroom, grabbed most of her clothes, shoes, and makeup, and left without saying another word.

A few days later she briefly returned to pick up more of her belongings. The divorce was not final for over a year, and in the interim she floated in and out of Samuel's life. Staying for a few days when she was insecure and out of money, she took advantage of his guilt and unwillingness to abandon her. The moment she felt inconvenienced, she would always leave. And Samuel would just wait. Alone.

The episode convinced him that he was truly alone in the world. He did not believe anybody could ever love him, and worse, he did not trust himself to search for that person.

Forced to face the demons of his life, he was too ashamed to reach for people that were capable of caring. He should have known there were people who loved him and had seen through his act all along. The only person Samuel had really fooled was himself.

He did such a good job of convincing himself that no one could help him, he unwittingly brought on the confrontation that would save his life. It was time for Samuel to suck up and face his demons.

And the demons did come, swarming him with nightmares, flashbacks, cold sweats, and worse. Afraid to close his eyes and battle his tormentors, more than once he went a week or more without sleeping. But what did he expect?

He was just a big fraud, and a loser.

THE PANIC OF LONELINESS

Nothing more than flesh

A body born to die

Put a bullet in my head

And I won't be afraid

When I close my eyes

HOLDING ON

A black forest of aged trees, tall and craggy, stands before me. It is barren of leaves, of birds, of anything. The sky is completely black, devoid of stars, the moon, or anything else. Clinging to an old broomstick, I am darting in and out of trees, bleeding from barbed branches that scrape across my body. They are as desperate to knock me off as I am to stay on, and after each blow I hear them groan. They're anguished, rabid to see me fall. Somehow I continue on.

Grasping the broom handle like a vise, my hands become numb. They are frozen into a steely grip, and that is good, because the broom begins to spin around, frantic to throw me off. I hold on, becoming dizzier and dizzier. Everything around me is blurred and confused except my one bit of hope, the thing I am chasing after - the light.

I can see it far away through the trees. Focusing on the light makes my ride bearable. The sting of the branches seems no more painful than tiny pinpricks, and the aching in my body can be ignored. I will make it to the light. I will hold on. But someone else has other ideas.

"Hah, hah, hah… I'll get you, boy!!"

I turn to see my pursuer, a witch; but she is not just some harmless comic-book sketch. Strong and determined, her face is hauntingly beautiful. With full lips, high cheekbones, and flowing black hair, she is intoxicating. An evil glare shoots forth from her coal black eyes, penetrating me like an optical dagger. Hunched down over her broom, her face and head are all I'm able to see.

"You will fall, boy!!" Screeching at me again, I am able to see her teeth. They gleam like diamond stilettos. How she would love to rip my flesh with them.

"You will not reach the light," she calls, reading my mind.

I do not answer her. I can't answer her. I so want the light. I must focus on the light. I must hold on.

"You will not reach the light."

"Ahh!!" Hit in the face with a branch the size of a bodybuilder's arm, I hear my nose crack, but I hold on.

"You will not reach the light."

The light is getting brighter now. I am drawing closer. I can almost feel its warmth. I've inched as far forward on the broom's handle as I can go. My head is sticking out well over the nub. I'm going to reach the light.

"You will not reach the light!"

I turn to look at the witch. Now I'm only able to see the top of her head. She is determined to stop me, but I am going to disappoint her. I am not going to give up. And anyway, I don't think I could let go if I wanted to, as cramped as my body is into this position of terminal clinginess.

"You will not reach the light!" she screams again.

This is one stubborn witch.

FAITH

A shadow dimly cast
Thin beam, a pale reflection

No fireworks
No trumpets sounded
No proclamation of truth

No poetry

Holding on to the only thing I could
Because there was nothing else

Samuel was indeed trying to hold on. The elves had quickly become a distant memory, and he was still falling – falling in a darkness that grew colder and darker.

"AAHH!!"

Further down the abyss he fell.

"Help me. Help me, God!!"

Falling, tumbling, he scratched wildly at the air.

"Mother, Mom...."

Deeper into the endless pit of darkness he dropped.

"God, hel... Ugh!"

Air rushed from Samuel's chest as his spent body impacted solid ground. Dazed, he could see nothing. But his mind was desperate to gather information. Filled with adrenaline, his senses were heightened to an edge where he could actually feel the glassy surface of his eyeballs sliding against the back of his eyelids.

He sat still on the floor waiting for his eyes to adjust to the darkness. For what seemed like an eternity, he waited and waited; but his surroundings only seemed to grow darker. Time, distance, space – all began to seem meaningless in this thick soup of blackness.

Samuel refused to believe he was alone. Desperate to prove it, he began to scamper along the ground like a blind man frantically searching for a dropped walking stick.

"Where am I?" he asked to no one in particular.

He began to become more than just frustrated. His crawl became quick and frenzied, probing deeper when...

Whamm!

He was jerked through the air by invisible tethers that tightly held his arms and legs. Samuel soon found himself strapped to an enormous concrete column. Stretched helplessly spread-eagle, as suddenly as he had been snared, his clothes vanished. Naked and freezing, shivering in the dark, the only thing starker than Samuel was the eerie silence.

Samuel's tortured mind yearned to scream, but his lips locked tight. Struggling against the tethers, joints aching, face straining, he thought to himself, "I must be in hell," or Bizarro World, because at that moment carnival music began to play, filling the silent void. From behind him a spotlight pierced the darkness. He quickly shut his eyes, which shielded him from the blinding glare. Gradually, he adjusted to the light and was able to see a large stage directly in front of him. Plain, not much more than a wooden platform, it was spanned by a large red curtain.

Suddenly the music stopped, but the steady beat of a bass drum continued as the curtain began to open. The unmasked stage floor revealed a group of young children. Milling about, giggling and laughing, they seemed oblivious to his presence.

Their activity halted as a small, naked child appeared on the stage. He was a twin of Samuel, from the glint of his blond hair and blue eyes to the fair complexion of his skin, but there was one great difference. This Little Samuel was conspicuously frail and feeble.

Conspicuous, that is, to anyone but Samuel. Although he had transformed his thin frame into one of sinewy strength and power, the figure kneeling on the stage was a familiar reflection.

Throughout Samuel's life, he had taken every opportunity to survey his appearance – a store window, a television screen, a bathroom mirror – but the figure never changed. He grew, but the weak child always remained, staring back at him.

And there he was again. Shivering uncontrollably, Little Samuel attempted to muffle his steady sobbing by wedging his head between his knees. Samuel wanted to reach out and cradle

70

him, but the tethers held firm. The harder he pulled, the tighter they became, and the harder Little Samuel seemed to cry.

Just as he finally gave up his straining, a gong sounded from somewhere behind the stage, and the children dispersed. Quickly forming a tight circle around Little Samuel, they smartly came to attention with solemn demeanors, their hands draped against their sides.

With an air of regalia, the largest boy in the group stepped forward, grabbed Little Samuel by the nape of his neck, and viciously jerked him to his feet. Little Samuel hung loosely from the boy's tight grip with only a hint of life left in his delicate body. He looked up at Samuel, and from Little Samuel's right eye a single tear fell down his soiled cheek.

"No, no...," Samuel cried. But what could he do? He couldn't even help himself.

Then a dagger appeared in the captor's free hand. This display of murderous steel broke the composure of the young audience. They began to salivate. Thick foam streamed through their grinding, gleaming teeth.

Samuel lost it.

While his taut muscles strained again against the tethers, he screamed at the stage's gathering storm.

"Stop it! Leave him alone, you bastards! Let me down or I'll...."

Samuel's demand was denied as the killer let loose a bloodthirsty scream while simultaneously raising his free hand high into the glare of the stage's spotlight.

"Die!!" he yelled.

The killer then looked over at Samuel. Flashing a crazed smirk, he struck. Faster than the spotlight's beam could reflect off the hardened steel, the dagger was thrust into Little Samuel's tiny chest. Its razor sharp blade entered without hesitation, violating his tender skin and thin ribs with ease. Little Samuel's eyes were wide and unbelieving. Nothing but silence filled his gaping mouth, and the only sign of life was the tear that still clung to his cheek.

Still hanging helplessly, Samuel prayed that shock had stopped the child's heart before the dagger plunged through. The killer could not have cared less. He pulled the knife from Little Samuel's chest, then nonchalantly wiped the dripping blade clean upon his ragged blue jeans. He chuckled and winked at Samuel. Casually, like a handyman discarding a dirty rag, he let Little Samuel's lifeless frame drop to the floor.

Samuel screamed a wailing cry of terror and disbelief. "No, no!"

But his words were cut short again. The killer, cheered on by the raucous shouting of the children, had hurled the blade toward Samuel.

Samuel struggled to increase the intensity of his scream, but silence was the only thing his terrified mind produced. The knife would enter his skull as easily as it had entered Little Samuel's flesh. He could see a drop of Little Samuel's blood hanging precariously on the tip of the blade. He was next.

Samuel was tired of fighting. He didn't struggle. He didn't move a bit. Like a stoic recipient of poetic justice, he wasn't even sure he wanted to try. After all, this bizarre drama might end his misery forever.

SEAR AND BURN

The sun's rays warm
The blooming meadow
Smiling toward the sky
Upon this quilt
Of yellows and greens
I lie

Into the heavens, I dream
Its rays begin to sear and burn
The flowers frown, their colors turn
To rise and run, would stall my fate

But like the meadow
Planted firm
I allow the sun
To sear and burn

Storms Revisited

For months as Samuel lay in his house recovering from the accident, everyone, including himself, did their best to ignore the severity of his injuries. No one from the command checked to see how he was doing; not even a chaplain visited, and no one from his family came to stay with him. They all figured, "Samuel is a stud, one of the best; he'll be all right."

But they were all wrong. As the days wore on, Samuel slept less, worried more, and sank deeper and deeper into corners of his mind that he had not known existed.

It was late on a Wednesday night, and he had not slept for two days. He did not know it, but the onset of severe insomnia was drawing near. Rather than lie in bed any longer, he put on some clothes and drove to a nearby gas station to fill up his car and get some snacks.

As he pulled up and started to pump, nothing seemed unusual. But then the gas fumes hit. Samuel was transported to the cockpit of his burning plane, and he could not escape – he was screaming, and he could feel the flames licking his face.

"Sir, sir, stop!" the gas attendant yelled. Samuel was standing in a daze as gas poured from the filled-up tank. But Samuel held the lever tight as the attendant yelled again and tried to unclench Samuel's hand and stop the dangerous flow of gas.

"Stop!!!" he screamed again, and Samuel finally woke from his flashback.

"Huh, what? Shit!" Samuel mumbled then cursed as he realized what had just happened. Embarrassed, he handed the attendant twenty dollars and drove home. As he pulled up in his driveway and turned off the ignition, pain consumed him, and he began to weep. For almost two hours he sat there in the darkness as tears streamed down his face.

A few days later Samuel was in the base medical center to have his back checked when he entered an elevator. He was already nervously awaiting the visit, fearful of the doctor's prognosis, when suddenly the elevator jerked upward.

Everything went black and Samuel was back in the Buckeye. Fire engulfed him and he writhed in the cockpit, screaming, burning to death. Through the intercom in his helmet, he could hear Lieutenant Skinner screaming at him.

"You're killing us, you child!" Lieutenant Skinner admonished.

"Ah, ahh!" Samuel howled in pain. "Let me die! Let me die! Let me..."

"Sir, sir, it's all right, sir, you're here at the hospital and everything is all right," a nurse assured Samuel as she cradled him on the floor of the elevator. Within seconds more help arrived, and after putting him in a wheelchair they took him to a room where he could recover. But as he stared at the white walls of the hospital room, all he could do was shake in fear.

Later that day, they released Samuel and he drove home, still in shock from the episode. They should have kept him longer, but they mistakenly thought his episode was a result of dehydration and had given him an IV. They figured that was enough.

After arriving home, Samuel went straight to the safe in his bedroom closet and removed his Smith and Wesson automatic. He checked to make sure it was loaded, which it was, and then lay down in his bed. He wanted to die. He put the gun to his head.

As the barrel of the pistol ground deep into his temple,

the accident flashed back repeatedly, interrupted only by visions of a little boy dreaming to fly. But the pistol brought him sick comfort, and after spotting his pillow with blood dripping from where the pistol had broken skin, he was asleep – asleep for the first time in almost a week.

For the next few months, he could count on the pistol to provide rest, but eventually the nightmares and fear overcame him, and sleep was only something that came after night upon night of bitter wakefulness – night upon night, coveting the power of the pistol, coveting the sweet release it could provide as the nightmares, hallucinations, pain, and fear grew worse.

BOXER

When did the curtain fall
On child light so burning bright
And when did the sparkle fade
The smile of stars cut free with a blade

One blow at a time, that's when
On the canvas now, the echoing count
Waiting to finish him

AGE SIX - I WANT TO READ

Samuel, age six, sat anxiously on the edge of his family's living room couch, unaware he was listening to what would be a momentous phone call. His mother was talking to his first grade teacher, Miss Summerall. This had been Samuel's second day in the first grade, and his concerned teacher had just called with some news. As they talked, Samuel sat with his face in his hands. Drooping limply toward the ground, his skinny legs hung off the edge of the sofa he was sitting on.

"Yes, I understand. No, he definitely can't. I will talk to him, and thanks for calling, Miss Summerall."

Shaking her head as she hung up the phone, Samuel's mother walked over from the phone and took a seat next to Samuel. After putting her arm around his shoulders, she lovingly grabbed his chin and pulled his little face towards hers. As sad as he was, Samuel's blue eyes still sparkled like a mountain brook. It broke her heart.

"Miss Summerall said you told her you could read. She also said that you insist on staying with the group of boys and girls that can read. I know you can't read, Samuel. Tomorrow you have to let Miss Summerall put you in one of the other groups."

"But I can read. I can," Samuel pleaded, choking back a tear.

"Samuel, it's okay that you can't read yet. Lots of girls and boys your age can't read."

"But I can read. I can read," Samuel began to sob in his mother's lap. He didn't want to go to school if he couldn't read. He was sure the kids would laugh at him.

His mother wanted to help her little boy, but all she could do was pat his back and tell him it would all be all right. Lying in bed later that night she said a little prayer.

"Please, Jesus, don't let my little boy be hurt too badly tomorrow. Miss Summerall is going to make Samuel go with one of the other groups, and it will break his little heart."

She would never know that Samuel had been in his bedroom praying. Kneeling on the floor next to his bed, he talked to Lord Jesus. For almost an hour he repeated a simple wish.

"Please, Jesus, let me read. Let me read."

The next day Samuel's mother cooked him a big breakfast of bacon and eggs. With a full stomach rumbling with anxiety, Samuel left for school. The school bus ride felt like a cattle car herding him toward a confrontation with Miss Summerall.

As the bus pulled into the school's parking lot, the pain in Samuel's stomach reached a crescendo. He was sure he was going to throw up. But like an answered prayer, as he walked into school and then down the hallway toward his classroom, the pain turned into the same comforting heat he would feel again years later right before leaping off his porch.

Walking into class, he didn't even have time to take his coat off before Miss Summerall approached him.

"Samuel, today you're gonna have to go with one of the other groups. I talked to your mother last night and she said she'd speak with you about it." Miss Summerall was bent over, resting on the balls of her feet, looking directly into Samuel's wide eyes.

"I know, ma'am. But I can read," Samuel spoke, pleading with Miss Summerall.

"Samuel, don't make this hard, son. If you keep refusing

to switch groups, I'll have to call your mother here from school. She'll be mad if I have to disturb her at work."

Her hands were on his shoulders now. She didn't want this to be difficult.

"But I can read," he assured her. "Give me a book and I'll show you."

Miss Summerall half-breathed a sigh of relief, figuring she finally could get this over with.

"All right, Samuel, but this is it. After you try, you're going to one of the other groups. Please don't make this any harder than it already is."

Miss Summerall quickly grabbed a first-grade reader and handed it to Samuel. He opened the worn book to the first page and began to stare at the words in front of him. He had never read before, but the warm throb was still comforting him. He knew he could read.

And read he did. Like a ray of sunshine penetrating a cloudy sky, the words came forth. Slowly, one at a time, and awkwardly pronounced, but indeed they came.

"See...Dick...ru...run." And on he went for a few more sentences. Miss Summerall was stunned.

"Very good, Samuel. I, I guess I'll let you give the reading group a try." She had never seen anything like it. That evening she called Samuel's mother and was assured that Samuel had never read anything before this.

In only a few weeks Samuel caught up and surpassed most of the other children. Nothing more was said about the incident. As the years passed both Miss Summerall and Samuel's mother would toss their heads and smile, thinking about that stubborn little child. How had he done it?

Samuel too would never forget those first words, or where

he had spent the night before – on his knees, praying. It was a lesson he would never forget, and a lesson that in his darkest hour would save him.

16 MONTHS AFTER LT. SKINNER'S DEATH

Kingsville, Texas

"What the hell?" Samuel wondered. He was lying in bed reading Jimmy Jones's *The Coming Armageddon Of Mankind* when he heard a loud shuffling sound from his living room. His continuing back pain and post-traumatic stress disorder kept him grounded, and the command had little for him to do while they decided whether to disability discharge him or not, so he had lots of free time on his hands, and a lot of that free time was spent exploring Bible prophecy and other supernatural literature.

Night after night of insomnia and the frequent flashback episode had left Samuel with few answers and little hope. The Marines had eventually thought it was best to have Samuel recover somewhere other than Meridian. Meridian didn't have appropriate medical facilities, and everyone thought a change of environment once he recovered would be a good idea. So after about four months in Meridian, he had spent six more at Pensacola, Florida, recovering, then when the military had deemed him fit for duty, they had sent him to Kingsville, Texas, to continue his training.

Ground school went well, but on Samuel's first flight he experienced severe back pain, his bladder emptied into his flightsuit on a maneuver and subsequent tests and an MRI showed that there was nerve damage that had not been discovered before. But his most severe damage wasn't to his back; it was to his soul, and he was about to discover just how serious it was really was.

"I must be crazy," he mumbled as he pulled back the sheets, rose from his bed, and shuffled off to investigate the sound he had just heard.

"That's strange," he muttered, extremely puzzled as he entered his living room. Samuel owned a Siberian husky and a Great Pyrenees. Surprisingly, the dogs were sound asleep and turned over on their backs with all of their furry legs spread wide and perfectly still. They were both hypersensitive dogs and would wake when a car passed by in the street. But they had obviously not heard the sound. In fact, nothing in the room seemed disturbed.

Scratching his head, Samuel figured he must be hearing things. He shuffled back to his room satisfied that nothing was amiss and eager to continue reading chapter three of *The Coming Armageddon Of Mankind*, "The Secret Identity of the Anti-Christ."

A few minutes later he heard the same noise again, but this time it was a good deal louder.

"Damn it all," he muttered again.

With a bit more vigor than before, he rose from bed, threw back the sheets, and marched into the living room. Once again, nothing was unsettled. Both dogs seemed to be dreaming. They lay flat on their sides emitting dim whines. Cody, the husky, was moving his paws frantically after what was probably a herd of cat-sized squirrels, while the Pyrenees, Molly, moved her paws at more of a gait. She was no doubt on some mountain patrolling for marauding grizzlies.

Puzzled and not nearly as satisfied as his dogs, Samuel unlocked his front door and stepped out onto his patio. The night was calm. A bank of dark, gray clouds hung not twenty feet above the few trees decorating his front yard. The street in front of his house was barren except for a few parked cars and scattered bits of trash. None of the neighborhood dogs were barking, and a few birds could be heard chirping peacefully. With nothing suspicious in sight, he returned inside, locked the door, and laughed at his wild imagination.

"But, my God," he said aloud while scratching his head again. "I heard something."

After checking the dead bolt one more time, he walked off to bed. Settling under his covers, Samuel checked his clock. It read 1:03 a.m.

"Damn, I better try to sleep," he mumbled to himself.

Frustrated at allowing another night to slip away, he reached for the light switch when, smack! He heard the same shuffling sound again. This third interruption was no charm. Pissed off, he reached to pull back his sheets when suddenly the air grew heavy. At first it just weighed him down, but in seconds it became a powerful living mass that effortlessly stretched his body straight as a board.

Panicked, Samuel tried to scream, but the organism of fear that surrounded him held his lips shut. When he tried to open his eyes and see his captor they were as locked tight as his mouth. Next, the same blanket of air holding his body forced his own hands around his throat. They began to choke him unmercifully. His mind became a mess of mindless activity. Unable to think straight, his brain filled with a thick soup of fear. All the emotions Samuel had spent a lifetime running from became his only reality: fear, death, panic, loneliness, and helplessness. They taunted him, dancing in his head like an annoying jester.

The beast gave Samuel no quarter. Forced into a corner of nightmares like some wild animal, his only chance for survival was to fight. Sweat poured out of his skin, and his heart was beating like the pistons of a two-hundred-mile-an-hour race car. He expected a heart valve to burst at any moment. Like a drugged hamster in a scientist's cage, he was frantically running to an acid infinity. If he couldn't gain control of himself, he knew he would die. But how?

The "how" was a voice that penetrated through the fog and shadows. It was his Uncle Tommy. He had been a spiritual mentor throughout Samuel's life.

"When full of fear and faced with evil, Samuel, pray. It's your best weapon."

Samuel attempted to follow these simple instructions, but each time he attempted a prayer, his thoughts became scrambled and confused. The words of the prayer would appear in his head looking like "Edar dlor lphe em." This obviously didn't have the same effect as if he had been able to say "Dear lord help me." Instead, his split-dyslexic plea only served to frighten him more.

Complicating matters was the grip around his throat that continued to grow tighter. He gasped for breath through pinched lips and snot-clogged nostrils. Sweat soaked his bed. This, combined with the immense heat generated by his feverish body, filled the room with the pungent smell of sick and musty flesh.

Samuel began to wish for a deathly release. Exhausted, no longer hysterical, he was ready to go and unsure of how much longer he could fight. Just as he was about to let the demon hands crush his larynx, he once again found an answer in the shadows. It was a Bible verse learned long ago, the 40th Psalm. It quietly called to him as clear as a mountain stream. As he spoke the words he could remember the faith of a little boy all those years ago – faith that had given him the strength to meet the challenge of his mother and teacher and read.

I waited patiently for the Lord;
he inclined and heard my cry.
He drew me from the desolate pit,
out of the miry clay.
He set my feet upon a rock,
and made my footsteps firm.

Slowly, one syllable at a time broke through the haze of his mind.

"I wai... wait... waited..." One word, then another, and soon the verse was repeating itself over and over.

The grip of his hands held, and the air still hung heavy. But slowly his mind began to clear like the passing of a storm. A little soggy, a little shell-shocked, it was clearing nonetheless.

He began to pray.

"Please, Lord Jesus, release me." Still unable to speak, the words echoed in his head. Just like mother had taught him, he prayed to Lord Jesus.

"Please, Lord Jesus..."

And prayed.

"Please, Lord Jesus…" Then suddenly his hands dropped from his throat. Eerily, his fingers stayed curled in their death grip of cramped muscles, aching bones, and strained tendons. He still couldn't move, but the air continued to thin. He could even begin to feel a cool breeze coming from the fan above him.

"Ple... Plea... Pleas..." Samuel struggled to pray aloud through pursed lips, fighting for every letter. He fought, refusing to surrender until his simple request could be invoked – one first invoked long ago by a little boy.

"Please, Lord Jesus, help me."

Over and over he repeated this simple phrase, fighting weakness, fear, and the doubt that he'd find and receive help. Then just as suddenly as it had trapped him, he felt the air lift from his body. Finally, he could move again.

"I've won," he thought to himself, "I've beat the demon." Then he opened his eyes.

He should have screamed at the figure that greeted him. But he lay still, as if he had expected to see it. A thin line of tears streamed down the expressionless features of Samuel's face. His blue eyes were opened just slightly, and his skin had the red glow one gets after a hot shower or long hard run.

Hovering above the foot of his bed was a syrupy demon whirling like some purple and black storm cloud. Atop this violent form was a bald head wearing the all too familiar face of Lieutenant Skinner that haunted his dreams. He looked panicked, and his mouth was open in a toothless, silent cry. Deep wrinkles lined the demon's face while tears streamed down both of his pale cheeks.

The demon spoke; his voice was loud, metallic, and familiar, like Lieutenant Skinner speaking through shards of aluminum.

"You killed me!!" he taunted, and Samuel just stared. "You killed me, why don't you just end your misery, you loser." The demon smirked and continued, "You were too scared to pull the ejection handle, and if you had just pulled it sooner I'd be alive. But you waited, and I had to pull it, and I died while YOU lived."

"You LIAR!!!" Samuel screamed. The demon was repeating the assertions of the accident board that had investigated the crash. When they could not find anything mechanical, they did whatever they could to blame the pilots, even though Samuel remembered something entirely different. But they could not have been too confident in their assertions. They still cleared Samuel to continue his training as soon as he healed from the accident. But he would not heal, and he would eventually be categorized as "physically unfit for duty" and given an honorable disability discharge.

"No, you killed me, you weak, pathetic little boy." The demon grinned and licked his lips.

"You liar!" Samuel screamed again. "Go back to where you came from!" Samuel was now bold and unafraid – unafraid for the first time since the accident.

"Go back," Samuel continued, "Go back and tell them I'm gonna win. You're not gonna beat me."

The demon clenched his jaw and began to reach for Samuel with a dry, leathered hand, when without explanation he turned and flew out Samuel's door into the night. It was as if he had been pulled away by an invisible hand.

Exhausted, Samuel's first reaction was to look at his clock. Its bright red numbers read 3:00 a.m. Two hours of madness were over. Tears still clung to his face, yet Samuel somehow felt satisfied, even fearless, in spite of the demon's guilty taunts.

"I am a winner," he told himself. What exactly he had won, though, he didn't know. Or did he?

"My life, I suppose," he mumbled aloud, remembering what had been the final inscription on the Air Force psychiatrist's consult form written a few months before – "HIGH SUICIDE RISK- WILL PROBABLY KILL HIMSELF IN 90 DAYS." It had been sent to his squadron, and Samuel had been forced to sit across from his commanding officer and hear the condemning words.

"The shrink here says you are a high suicide risk. Now

that's just talk, isn't it, son?" No, it was not just talk. But of course Samuel didn't say that.

"Yes, sir. I'm one hundred percent. Don't worry about me, I'll get better."

I AWAKE TO GHOSTS

Demon, slayer

Cruel, soul-taker

Spiderwebs invade my mind

Hallucinate

A spirit steals

Life, one dream at a time

This blood drip ghost

And a red tear pleads

Forgive me

Forget me

Free me

WHO AM I?

The magical journey continued, and Samuel lay curled like a sleeping infant frozen in a bizarre image. His eyes were wide and crazy, his mouth stretched and strained into the terrified scream of a man being burned alive.

But he was far from any inferno – just the opposite. He lay upon a lone white cloud ten thousand feet above the earth, a puffy speck in a deep blue sky.

As he settled into the comfort of the pillowy cloud, he fell into the half-awake, dreamy fringe of sleep. Like those precious moments found during lazy Saturday mornings in bed, he was in no hurry to rise. And besides, there was no telling what lurked behind closed eyelids.

"Yes," he thought to himself, "I'll just lie here."

Or so he hoped. A voice, gentle and unassuming, startled him with a simple greeting.

"Hello there, Samuel. My name is Jeremy."

Samuel woke from his daze and looked to see an angel. Like some storybook cliché, he stood tall with a long white gown. His wings were tucked neatly behind his back, and a large warm smile glowed beneath a golden head of hair.

"What are you? Some angel?" Samuel paused and then bitterly continued. "You're a lifetime late. Who slipped a freak like you into this sick dream?"

"Samuel, Samuel, my boy, you are not dreaming. I've been here your entire life waiting to reveal myself," Jeremy answered, a whimsical look appearing on his face. "And yes, I guess you could call me an angel. I prefer Jeremy, though. Freak is a little hard, don't you think?"

Samuel was in no mood for beating around the bush with a wisenheimer, white-winged angel. He wanted some answers and at the moment could not care less what Jeremy liked to be called.

"Maybe you are an angel," Samuel considered since they were standing on a cloud. "But who were those people before, and what am I doing here? I'm sick of being tossed around."

Samuel was already a bit exasperated. So when a large, brown leather chair appeared, instantly occupied by Jeremy, he made no effort to hide his impatience and disdain.

"Am I supposed to be impressed?" Samuel glared.

"Why, Samuel?" Jeremy began. "No one is trying to impress you. When you leaped off your porch you did not seem too concerned about where you were going. You flew. Now stop worrying and enjoy the ride. Do you see anyone else lounging around up here?"

Samuel squirmed, a bit unsettled by the mini-lecture. He was sure of nothing but his frustration.

"No, but do you see anyone else watching their heart get ripped out, tumbling around like a freaking box of rocks? I want to know what the hell I'm doing. Whose big idea was this...," Samuel hesitated, increasingly awed by the majesty of his lofty perch. This wonder tempered his vehemence as he continued. "And why the hell am I on this cloud?"

Jeremy, compassion filling his eyes, sat up in his chair and looked down at Samuel. "I can't say, Samuel. It's not my place."

"What do you mean, you can't say? What's the point then? Am I some game?!" Samuel fired up again. He was about ready to jump off the cloud with or without Jeremy's help.

"The point," Jeremy continued, "is that you are ALMOST ready to fly. Real flying, without any help from me."

"Fly! I thought I was flying. What are you talking about, real flying?"

"All in time, Samuel. All in time."

Jeremy tried to sound encouraging, but Samuel just fired

back insolently.

"All in time," he smirked. "That's sure easy for you to say. You are an angel, you got all the time in the world."

"It's not the time, Samuel; it's the perspective. I see your life through the eyes of God."

"Eyes of God?" Samuel raised a wary eyebrow. This was getting a little too preachy for him.

"That's right. Your pain seems great to you, and it is, but measured against eternity, the worst of your torment is like a bump on a two-year-old's knee. The parents may be concerned at the time, but years later they see it as nothing more than a fond memory of their little boy growing up. You are growing up, whether you realize it or not."

Samuel had stopped paying attention after hearing "eyes of God" and was dangling his feet over the edge of the cloud while he stared down at the ground thousands of feet below. Jeremy did not find this amusing.

"Listen, my boy. You've been dangling your feet long enough. That's no way to find the answers to any of your questions."

"Answers, yeah, how 'bout some answers?" Samuel rose to his feet and approached Jeremy's chair with his hands resting defiantly on each hip.

"Why am I flying? Did you forget that little request? That little question, your angelness? Save your God mumbo jumbo for someone else."

Jeremy smiled, wondering how a boy on a cloud, talking with an angel, could characterize talk of God as mumbo jumbo.

"The only sucker, Samuel, is the man hiding from himself and the truth of his existence. It's not my job to tell you all the answers. I am only here now to assure you. You're flying and when you're ready to go home, you will. Please remember, I'll always be close."

And with that Jeremy vanished.

YOU WILL

A face in the mirror appeared to me
A familiar mask with a familiar plea
It's late, I'm tired, I need to sleep
Let me fall, this tattered heap

NO!!

It screams, I'm terrified
Sleep is an ocean, too far and wide
To cross to tomorrow, that I cannot bear
To wake to the horror, another day of despair

So I sit a little longer and try to find
The question, the answer, that escapes my mind
But all that remains when the night fades away
My desperate cry and my weary face

"Wait, wait –," Samuel yelled as he lunged towards Jeremy's empty throne.

"I wanna –"

Whoooooooshh!! The cloud disappeared.

"Noo!!" Samuel pleaded, falling through the sky. The ground rushed toward him, clearer and closer, dizzyingly fast.

He tumbled, screaming, cursing, and crying for help as a voice broke through the chaos.

"Fly, Samuel," Jeremy's reassuring words echoed in the wind, "I am with you."

"Where, where are you?" Samuel was no longer angry with Jeremy; he just wanted his help.

"Right here, where I've always been. Now fly."

So Samuel did. With nervous eyes, his body tense, Samuel's arms and legs opened wide, sharply catching the wind. He flew, soaring once again.

16 Months and a Day After the Accident

The afternoon after his encounter with the demon, Samuel was sitting in his living room, bored and tired of petting his dogs while reading apocalyptic musings. It was then that he decided to fulfill a lifelong desire and learn to play guitar. Having written poems as a child, he figured mastering a few chords could possibly lead to writing songs. So after grabbing some jeans and a wrinkled shirt off his floor, he headed down the street for a local music shop he had been driving by for months.

Alfred's music store had been in business for over fifty years, and from the looks of the dusty shelves, still had some original inventory. As Samuel pushed through the old glass front door, he was greeted by a balding forty-year-old with a stringy grey ponytail hanging down his back. Samuel recognized him from the local bar, where the man's band, the Aces, played everything from Lynyrd Skynyrd to Metallica, but mostly Lynyrd Skynyrd.

"Hey, I've seen you down at the Wild Boar Saloon," The man recognized Samuel. "My name is Kurt, what can I help you with?" he asked genuinely.

"Well, I've always wanted to play guitar, so I figured today was a good day to start." Samuel spoke slowly, he seemed very determined.

"Well," Kurt answered, "I guess ya better start with an acoustic, and you'll probably need some kinda book to start with."

Samuel eyed the store and noticed a display of acoustic guitars with SALE stickers. A dark brown one caught his eye. The price was right, so he grabbed it and asked for Kurt's recommendation on songbooks.

"What do you think I should get to learn with?" Samuel asked.

"Well, usually I tell people to get a songbook of a group they like. It makes the learning more motivating. We got a whole section of songbooks with easy chords so you can learn the songs faster. What band do you like?" Kurt asked.

It only took Samuel a split second to reply, "I like The Beatles." He could still remember staying up to watch the *Yellow Submarine* cartoon on TV.

"Well, here ya go," Kurt grabbed a thick songbook. "It's the *Easy Beatles* songbook. The beginning tells you how to play the chords, and above the lyrics of each song are the chords for each part. You know the melody, so just strum and follow along as best you can." Kurt made it sound easy.

"All right, then, how much do I owe you?" Samuel pulled out his wallet.

"How about ninety-nine dollars plus tax – I'll throw the songbook in for free." Kurt smiled. Samuel then plopped down cash, took his change, and headed out the door with his guitar and an innocent smile.

Once home, Samuel began his task. Opening the book to what looked like one of the easier songs, *Hey Jude*, he began to awkwardly finger chords and even more awkwardly sing. He loved it. Day after day he would sit on his sofa and strum the guitar, keeping company with the Beatles. Still unsettled and vulnerable in the aftermath of his accident, it was all he looked forward to each day and most nights.

Soon the songbook was dog-eared from use, and Samuel was writing his own songs, making his own music. From that point on, whenever life became unbearable, Samuel would find refuge with his songs. It was a thirst for creativity he had felt before.

AGE 9 - ON A CLOUD

Little Samuel was alone in Miss Lauderdale's third-grade class sitting quietly between a large bookshelf and the back wall of the classroom. He had in his hands a jumbo-sized pencil and a standard-issue, wide-ruled writing notebook. Working diligently, his head was bent over in furious concentration that left his face less than a foot from the page.

He wrote carefully, correcting words with his rectangular eraser after practically every sentence. He was so entirely engrossed, in fact, that he didn't notice Miss Lauderdale when she walked over to him and began looking down over the bookshelf onto his notebook. Samuel couldn't help but jump when she finally spoke.

"Whatcha writing, Samuel?" she smiled, bending closer, resting her hands on her knees.

"Oh, just a story." Samuel shrugged.

"A story? What is it about?"

"You know, knights, dragons, and stuff. I think someday I'm gonna go where King Arthur and his knights lived," Samuel smiled.

"Knights and dragons, sounds like fun," she smiled back.

"I guess so," Samuel replied and then looked back down at his tablet. In less than a second he was writing again.

"Why don't you let me look at your story, Samuel. I especially like knights."

"It's not finished," Samuel curtly replied, not even looking up from his work.

"Well, that's okay, maybe I can help a little."

"I don't think so. I like to write alone. But, uh, I do have another one that I have finished."

100

He handed Miss Lauderdale a second notepad that was lying on the floor next to him. He explained a little as he handed it to her, "It's not really a story. It's a fairy tale."

"Whatever it is, Samuel, I am sure that I will like it." Grabbing the tablet from Samuel she began to read.

A MAN ON A CLOUD

Once there was a man named Clyde and he lived on a cloud. He liked it and he wanted something to drink. He made a well in the cloud. But he was very lonely. He wanted a wife but he didn't know how to get to earth. Then he had an idea. He would build a spaceship. It took him from October to November. Finally it was done and he looked for a wife at Mars. Right before his eyes he saw the woman to be his wife. Her name was Judy. He asked Judy to be his wife and she said yes. And he wasn't lonely any more. The End

Miss Lauderdale paused for a minute after she finished reading. The short tale unsettled her, but she couldn't figure out exactly why. She wondered what loneliness lurked in the little dreamer working away in front of her.

"What did ya think?" Samuel asked, noticing she was not reading any more.

"That was just great, Samuel. Keep it up and you might just be a writer someday." She did her best to sound encouraging.

"I wanna be a fighter pilot," Samuel stated assuredly.

"A fighter pilot? Why a fighter pilot, Samuel? Why not a

writer?" Miss Lauderdale couldn't help but look surprised. The frail little boy in front of her did not look like a future fighter pilot.

"Well, it's not as cool. Everyone says I'll grow up to be something like a fighter pilot. I told them I wanted to be like, um, Ernest Emingway," Miss Lauderdale smiled at his awkward pronunciation of 'Ernest Hemingway.' "And they just smiled at me. They said how hard it was to please the people who make books."

"I think Mom and Dad want me to be like my uncles who were fighter pilots in World War Two. They gave me books with Air Force planes and pilots in it." In reality they didn't, but powerful images impact children powerfully.

"That would be nice, Samuel, but do you want to be a fighter pilot?"

"I guess so. It sure looks cool, and nobody messes with fighter pilots."

"But don't you stop writing. Maybe someday those people that make books – they are called publishers – will send you a nice letter." She wanted to be encouraging.

"That would be neat," Samuel smiled.

"Yeah, that would be neat," Miss Lauderdale replied, flashing Samuel a warm grin. Silently, she prayed that the shiny things of this world wouldn't make the dreams of a small child their own.

A RAMBLING DREAMER: REMEMBER ME

The sound of my feet, running from one dream to the next
Is killing me

Wandering away from failure, the only rewards I collect
Are those I fall upon

Fake, Fake, Fake, Fake, Fake, Fake, Fake

My steps are getting slower now, new dreams harder to find
I am tired of dreaming

Turning to dust in my steel coffin, I'll be laughing
As people remember the dreamer

But that was the third grade. Today Samuel was flying. He had been given the opportunity to soar again by Jeremy, and he took it. Aerial bravery quickly surfaced, and Samuel headed for the ground in another hypersonic dive. He glowed, a young lord of gravity.

Nearing the earth, he eyed a cabin nestled among a small grove of trees. Fear caused him to hesitate, but curiosity convinced him otherwise. He flew toward the cabin, and a closer inspection revealed it to be a simple structure. A hasty combination of rotten wood sheets and a warped tin roof, it was covered with dirt and grime. Samuel wanted to know what was inside. He landed next to it and wiped clean one of its filthy windows, since there seemed to be no doors.

It revealed a single, simple room. Dominating the far wall was a large fireplace, dusty and unused. A pine table and two chairs were in the center of the room, but except for cobwebs, the rest of the cabin was bare.

Then suddenly, a boy appeared in the least stable of the wooden chairs. Little Samuel was back. He wore nothing but a soiled pair of tight briefs, which fit the Spartan surroundings well. With his arms dangling and his chin just centimeters from his chest, Little Samuel sobbed.

"Not again," Samuel thought. "Don't do this to him again."

Silent and apprehensive, Samuel's fear darkened as the source of the little one's torment appeared in the cabin. He remembered them well. They were a fat, ugly couple with jet black hair and oversized, decades-old polyester clothing. Acquaintances of Samuel's family, these slovenly people had visited infrequently, but memorably, throughout his lifetime.

Dangling from their hands were cigarettes that littered the floor with ashes and filled the air with a thick cloud of choking smoke. These were filthy people whose cruel words were just as disgusting. Samuel could hear their venom clearly through the window.

"Girls write diaries, Samuel, not boys," they both spoke, "I told your mother she was raising a sissy. Looks like we were right. I bet you're wearing dirty underwear, too, ya little creep." Their smoke-stained hands gestured wildly, holding Little Samuel's sacred diary as they cruelly invaded the sanctity and security of the only place he had ever thought it safe to be himself.

"It is so foolish, Samuel. Whining, complaining little rhymes," they mocked him, continuing to wave his diary like a television preacher with a ragged King James Version of the Bible.

"It's not stupid," Little Samuel muttered under his breath.

"Shut up, boy. You tell anyone about this and we'll say what's in this silly book. We'll tell everyone you sat here crying with crusty underpants." They spoke in unison, this devil and his witch.

"Please stop," Little Samuel cried.

"Shut up, boy!" SMACK, the woman slapped Samuel.

"But..." Samuel tried to plead again.

"Boy!" the man yelled and then spit on Samuel. "You give up that girly act or we'll treat you like a girl."

The attack continued, and Samuel slammed his fists against the window. Nothing happened, not even the dust moved. He turned to find a rock or anything that might break the glass, but his feet stayed planted to the ground. He was as powerless as the small boy within. He fell to his knees and cried.

When the maggots finally disappeared, two defeated souls were left behind. Little Samuel's diary, thrown on the floor, was already gathering dust. It would never be written in again, and Little Samuel would soon begin to forget what precious words had been put there.

Samuel began to rage. He rose with his fists balled tight and cursed Jeremy. "You fake!! Why did you even give me hope? Damn you and damn your God!" As his eyes glared skyward, Samuel wanted nothing less than to find Jeremy and incinerate him.

BLIND MAN'S PSALM

God above and man below
How does this order really go

Life of chaos, strange working fate
Where is reason, oh God I hate

Leaned on you, your crutch it failed
Leaned on myself, my own cross I nailed

Circles and spirals, deeper, darker I go
Now nothing to stop me, the abyss down my hole

And I scream
Where are you God

Samuel stayed next to the cabin for hours, kneeling with his face buried deep in his hands. Ready to die if something would come and take him there, he had neither the energy nor will to do it himself. But his wish was denied. Instead, he felt himself placed in a chair. Weary and puzzled, he brought his head slowly up out of his hands and found himself seated behind a broad, wooden desk.

And in what seemed a proper exclamation point to his mystifying journey, he sat suspended in outer space. No moon, no earth, no sun – just the glow of a deep black sky filled with brilliantly radiating stars. Samuel could not help but chuckle.

"Nice touch."

He had not expected a reply, but he sure got one. In front of him an enormous mirror twice the size of the desk appeared. In it was a large, distorted image of a man's face covered with tears along with a tired look of loneliness and lost dreams. There was no mistaking to whom the reflection belonged. The face was his. Samuel was not flying any more.

Suddenly, overcome with despair, old questions a lifetime had never answered convulsed in his mind. "What have I been doing with my life? Who am I and why do I make such awful decisions? When I die, will I become nothing but fertilizer?"

He could have gone on, but one self-pitying query screamed louder than the rest: "When will I ever find peace?"

Samuel was spared from this self-loathing as a pen and paper materialized on the desk's surface, followed by an old, beaten guitar leaning against the side. They were accompanied by a familiar and unexpectedly welcome voice.

"Go ahead," Jeremy encouraged.

"What do you mean?" Samuel replied, his teary eyes deep and questioning.

"Ready for a lecture?" Jeremy's right brow bent upward.

"Sure. Where am I gonna go?" he quipped as he straightened up a little and wiped his eyes.

"Samuel, who you are and what you do are not the same. You let the disappointments of life define you. You could never stop and separate yourself from any of it.

"Life began to look smaller and smaller, your opportunities fewer and fewer. All of this because your self-worth was drawn from what you did and what you thought people saw you as. You wanted to be invincible, but in reality you became terminally insecure, afraid of shedding old, fraying but familiar clothes.

"Then your accident exposed the lies. It stripped you naked and forced you to look nowhere but inside. At first, the only thing you found was a wish to die. You wanted to kill yourself. After a lifetime of trying to prove to people you were strong and tough, you couldn't recognize the opportunity you had been given. Whether you liked it or not, you were going to face the truth of your life.

"You might have perished, but you fought, Samuel. You did not drown, and you did not give up. And now you are finally starting to see. The little boy who wrote poems and told stories wants to be free to grow up. You can only see life through the eyes of God when your soul stands bare. You are on your way, but the trip will continue to be scary. You have spent your entire life doing anything possible to be liked by everyone. You forgot one person – yourself."

A tear slowly dripped from Samuel's eye.

"Listen closely, son, you are standing naked in a reflective pool. Don't be in a hurry to wade back to shore for your clothes. Swim awhile and it won't take long to realize you never needed them in the first place."

Jeremy paused. Samuel didn't know how to reply, but he had a question.

"All those years ago in Iceland," he asked as he wiped the tear from his cheek, "was that you? Was that your voice? And my accident, was that you who carried me to the ground?"

Jeremy smiled, "It wasn't me."

"If it wasn't you, who was it?" Samuel whispered. He had been sure it was Jeremy.

"I'm not telling," Jeremy smiled again, "but I'm pretty sure you'll cross paths again."

Samuel wanted to reply, but he was too exhausted to talk anymore; he just wanted to rest.

"You'll fly, Samuel, just pick yourself up and fight for yourself. Live with passion. You should know as much as anyone that everyday is a gift to be lived. Write poems, play your guitar, explore the world, find love, and all that is important will reveal itself." As he finished, Jeremy touched Samuel for the first time and gave him a hug.

As his face buried in Jeremy's embrace, the simple voice of a child echoed in Samuel's head.

"Jeremy is right – it's time to fly."

FREEDOM

Twenty-eight months after Samuel's accident

Samuel was stretched out in an Air Force-issue green cushioned chair like an anxious schoolboy waiting to leave for summer break. Dr. Lisa Germano, U.S. Air Force psychiatrist, was trying her best to get him to pay attention. A few months after Samuel's encounter with the demon, he had finally revealed his flashbacks and insomnia to a base chaplain who had then referred Samuel for an evaluation. When the degree of Samuel's PTSD had been determined, he had been sent to Wilford Hall Medical Center in San Antonio, the finest aviation hospital in the armed forces, for treatment and further therapy for his back pain, which still lingered. After months of therapy it had finally been decided to grant Samuel a disability discharge; this would be his last meeting with his therapist, Dr. Germano.

"You're still wearing your flight suit," she observed. "I told you you didn't have to wear it unless you wanted."

"It's comfortable," he mumbled. As bright and talkative as Samuel could be, he still felt a little uncomfortable with Dr. Germano. It had been hard for the rough marine to fully accept her counseling.

"Sleeping any better?" she asked.

"A little." He reconsidered. "Actually, the last six months have been better and better. I went three nights in a row last week with sleep." Samuel smiled and for an instant his face lit up.

"Still talking to angels?" Dr. Germano asked half-seriously but respectfully. She had given up convincing Samuel they were basically hallucinations.

"Sure," he answered, remembering his last conversation

with Jeremy. "I don't think I'm gonna need to see him again, though." Then he reconsidered. "At least for a while."

"So I see your disability discharge was finalized." She moved on. "It's been a long time coming, over two years since your accident. That's lots of time to think. Any idea what you are going to do next?"

"I don't know. Maybe I'll travel. And I really want to keep working on my writing and guitar." He thought for a moment and then spoke. "I wrote a new song last night. It's pretty good." His face lit up again.

"Really?" Dr. Germano leaned forward in her chair. "Tell me about it."

"It's called *Bonnie and Clyde*." He grinned wider.

"*Bonnie and Clyde*?" She questioned back through a smile.

"Yeah, it's about a crazy couple who go on adventures together." He weakly smiled, then paused for a second before revealing, "You know, Doc, I'm tired of being alone." He coughed and wiped his mouth as a line of tears rolled down his cheek. "So tired."

Dr. Germano leaned forward and grabbed one of Samuel's massive shoulders. She waited, and once Samuel had wiped away the tears, she replied, "You're gonna make it, Samuel." A warm, thin smile broke across her face. "I've seen you come so far. The first time we met, I wasn't sure you were gonna survive. But you fought, and now I'm excited to see what paths you are gonna blaze."

"You really think so?" Samuel questioned through a smile as he regained his composure.

"Of course. I've read your poems, we've spent the last months talking about your dreams, examining your life, discovering who the real Samuel is." As she spoke, color and confidence appeared on his face. "All we've done is talk. You're the one who had the courage and strength to fight."

"I sure don't feel courageous," he replied sarcastically. "I must look like some joke sitting in here in my flight suit. I'll be a civilian in a few weeks."

"Stop it, marine!" she snapped and gave Samuel a gentle nudge. "Enough of that feeling sorry for yourself."

Samuel smiled and his back straightened. Looking into her eyes, he answered.

"I'll make it, Dr. Germano," he stated resolutely. "It's hard to deal with everything sometimes, but I think I know what my purpose is, and since the demon attack, I've been praying a lot – it really helps."

"Keep going," Dr. Germano led Samuel on.

"It seems like my poems really speak to people, and a lot of friends are encouraging me to write a book about my accident. I think I could help a lot of people. I can't be the only one who has suffered like this." Samuel reasoned.

"You are right about that." Dr. Germano agreed. "The hardest thing in the world to do is truthfully examine your life and then do something about what you find."

"Yeah," he answered. "Six months ago I wouldn't have believed that I would soon be leaving the Marines to walk the earth, write books, and make music," he commented proudly.

"So, I'm interested." Dr. Germano questioned him. "What do you want to say with your writing and music?"

"To never give up, to fight, to fight like a mother protecting her young," He paused. "And to be unafraid to listen to the voice God has put inside you. If you pray and listen, God will reveal a way. When he does, you must follow."

"You make that sound easy." She smiled, wondering who

was the teacher here.

"Well, I think God's voice is true. We just don't always like what he has to say, so we complicate matters in order to find alternate definitions. God gave me gifts. Poems pour from my heart, melodies ring in my head. How could it be any clearer?" He smiled confidently, almost daring her to disagree as his confidence grew.

"I guess it couldn't." She smiled, not totally convinced, but willing to believe.

Later that night, Samuel was back in his room praying. He held a well-worn prayer rope that he used to shuffle beads through his fingers as he recited the simplest prayer: "Lord Jesus Christ, Son of God, have mercy on me, a sinner."

While visions of pain could still fill his head, hallucinations could paralyze him, his back could ache unmercifully, and depression could creep over him at any moment, this prayer gave him the strength and focus to find peace and clarity

"Lord Jesus Christ...." The words would flow, and his mind would slowly drift away from his surroundings. It was as if a fog lifted and all before him would become clear. He could envision a simple life, a life attached to the pursuit of meaningful things, a life spent pursuing the creation of words and music and truth.

"...have mercy on me, a sinner." He would repeat it over and over again, losing track of time, occasionally through the night into the morning. It didn't take long for the mere thought of the words to penetrate his mind, stop the spiral of despair, and cut through with clarity and purpose.

He had found the prayer strolling through a Borders bookstore in a simple little book called *The Way of the Pilgrim*. It told of a Russian peasant who sought true prayer, and the "Jesus Prayer," as it was called, was what he found to be the answer. It had resonated with Samuel, and ever since he had adopted its practice. Almost immediately, he began to feel the presence of God – a presence missing since that day long ago in Iceland when he had been warned that he would suffer. Thankfully, now God's presence only helped to reassure him that he was on the right path – a path of spirit, and prayer, and following the dreams that had been placed in his heart so long ago. These dreams included a long motorcycle trip.

It was about a week since his last meeting with Dr. Germano and the day before his official discharge. Samuel had sold almost everything he owned. He had even found a home for his dogs on a farm near his parents in Indiana, and a couple weeks earlier had driven there and back to deliver them.

Under a blazing midday South Texas sun, he pulled up in his Porsche 944 Turbo to the local Kawasaki motorcycle dealer, where a flight surgeon from the base was waiting to purchase it from him.

"You'll enjoy it," Samuel said as he slammed the door of the 944 Turbo shut for Lieutenant Dale Daniel, the proud new owner of Samuel's red Porsche. Pleased, and with the selling price of cash in his hands, he walked into the showroom of the Kawasaki dealership as Lieutenant Daniel tore out of the parking in the last remnant of Samuel's false path.

Upon entering, a large on-/off-road enduro motorcycle caught his eye, the Kawasaki KLR 650. Large enough to cruise on the highway, built to go off road, it was the perfect bike for adventure. And in spite of the back pain Samuel knew prolonged riding would cause, he was more than ready for adventure.

As Samuel approached the salesman with cash in hand,

he was ready to buy. And he swaggered. The little boy inside swaggered again, ready to hit the road and soar. He had indeed suffered, but suffering had brought freedom, and a new journey was about to begin.

BERZI

Three years, three months, two weeks, three days since the accident
Eleven months since leaving the Marines and hitting the road

After parking his motorcycle in front of an old duplex just a couple blocks from Indiana University in Bloomington, Indiana, Samuel dismounted his Kawasaki KLR 650 motorcycle, then unfastened and took off his helmet, which revealed shoulder-length, dirty blond hair. After wiping his sweaty brow he headed inside, still swaggering from a trip that had taken him across Texas, through the plains states, and then home to Indiana.

Samuel was stopping in Bloomington to see an old high school friend's sister, Becky, who was a student at IU and was sure to have plenty of eligible, good-looking friends, Samuel assumed. As he strode into Becky's apartment, his faced was etched with a big smile and wide eyes at whatever potential adventure might lie ahead. Upon entering, though, he encountered something quite unexpected. The front door opened into the living room of Becky's apartment, where piled in the middle of the floor was an odd collection of clothes, schoolbooks, shoes, a backpack, and a long-haired, small black dog. Lying in the middle of the mess was a smiling coed adorned with a well-worn sundress, some black soccer shorts underneath, and an old pair of trail shoes.

"Hi, there!" Samuel smiled with a short wave as he walked in and set his backpack down on the floor.

"Hey," she let out a short reply and smiled.

"I'm Samuel. Is Becky around?" he queried as he surveyed the small apartment. "She was expecting me."

"I think she's still at class. I'm sure she'll be back soon." She kept smiling, then followed cheerfully, "There's drinks and some food in the fridge if you want."

"Thanks, I've been on the bike for hours, and I'm starving. " He headed toward the kitchen then paused to ask, "What's your name, anyway?"

"Berzi," She smiled.

"Berzi," he repeated back. "Well, pleased to meet you, Berzi"

With that Samuel walked back to Becky's kitchen where he grabbed a Corona from the fridge and waited for Becky to return so they could plan the night's activities. Back in the living room, still huddled amidst her pile of belongings, Berzi was in a bit different mood. Her world had been rocked. The moment Samuel had walked in and smiled at her, the hammer of destiny had fallen, and one thought rung in her head.

"That's the man I'm going to marry."

That was the last Berzi and Samuel saw of each other on this trip, but a few weeks later Samuel returned, and fate struck hard again. A large group was gathered in Becky's living room listening to lots of Oasis music. Becky's boyfriend's band had recently been signed by the manager of that great English band, Oasis, and everyone was in high spirits. So as the music played and drinks flowed, smiles bounced off the walls of the small apartment. Samuel even grabbed a guitar and loudly started to sing the multitude of Beatles songs he had learned since buying his guitar and Beatles songbook. It was something that Becky and her friends did not find amusing as the night drew on and the party tried to watch a movie while Samuel just sang louder and louder, oblivious to the disturbance he was creating. But as Becky and her friends smirked, Berzi just smiled at the comedy of it all.

As the evening wore on, Samuel was trying to remember an Elvis song when he called out to the party.

"Hey, guys, you know, I never got to visit to Graceland when I was in college at Vanderbilt. I have my parents' car – who wants to take off and visit Graceland? If we leave soon we could be there by morning."

"Awesome idea!" the entire party proclaimed. But by the end of the night, when Samuel was ready to saddle up and go, only one actually took him up on his offer: Berzi.

A little before midnight they headed out of Bloomington for the seven-hour drive to Graceland. It was a clear late-summer sky, and the stars sparkled as Samuel and Berzi hit the highway and sped from town. With the car's sunroof open, the wind blew back Berzi's hair, and they started to talk the night away.

"So what do you think about all those stars?" Berzi pondered, staring up through the sunroof.

"I think God did a good job." Samuel grinned. Berzi paused for a minute, then spoke.

"God – what do you think about God?"

"I think God created us because he could, and the point of life is to have a relationship with him."

"Relationship?" she replied, a bit incredulous, but intrigued. "What do you mean?"

"I mean I believe God created us with the same love that a couple has when they start having kids. He wants to love and protect us, but he also wants us to be our own person. And that only comes through pain, struggle, and the joy of following our own unique purpose. Life is like a fire – it can eat you up or turn you into something stronger and better than you ever imagined."

And on they talked, speaking of the mysteries of the universe, favorite bands, books, and funny personal stories. At one point, though, during a long moment of silence, Samuel looked up through the sunroof and was sure he saw ole Jeremy sitting near a star with a big smile on his face. That was enough to convince Samuel that his path was clear and God's plan for his life was straight ahead. With a wink Jeremy disappeared, and a tear slid down Samuel's happy face.

By 7:00 a.m. they were at Graceland, and joining them in the parking lot was a bus load of Japanese tourists.

"Japanese tourists? Can you believe it?" Samuel laughed.

"I don't know if anyone back in Bloomington would believe me even if I took a picture," Berzi said as she grabbed his hand and they headed for the entrance to Graceland.

After the Graceland trip, Samuel was able to visit a couple more times, and with each interlude their adventures grew more diverse. There was hiking, biking, long coffee shop discussions, and a whole lot of Samuel trying to write songs that would meet Berzi's approval. In early September, the trip which would seal their fate together coalesced.

Samuel had wanted to get back out on the road for a while, and he figured if he left now he would have time to visit Yellowstone National Park before winter set in. But he didn't want to leave without a goodbye to Berzi. So he headed south to Bloomington, where she was just starting her semester, before he traveled west on another epic journey.

As he rode up to her apartment, she was able to hear the motorcycle approaching and ran outside to great him.

"Hey, there! You look like you are ready for some fun!" she exclaimed with an enormous smile stretched across her face.

"Yep, got my tent, sleeping bag, some cooking supplies." Samuel patted the pack strapped behind him. "About everything

I'll need for the road. Why that big smile on your face?"

"Oh, I've got some news of my own. I've decided to take the semester off and go visit some family out in Colorado." Berzi proudly explained.

"Family in Colorado? You should just come with me." Samuel began to persuade her.

"Whatever." She flipped her eyes back.

"Hey, we'll visit Yellowstone, Devil's Tower, Mount Rushmore, the Badlands, the Tetons, the Grand Canyon, and we'll finish up at my Grandma Toodles, where we can ski, swim, and drink her world-famous sweet tea!"

"I'll think about it, crazy!" She pushed him on the shoulder and smiled, but the wheels of fate were set in motion.

She didn't have to think long, and the next day they hit the road for the adventure of a lifetime and the beginning of their life together.

PEACE

I had a dream last night. I was sitting in a field of wild, rainbow-colored flowers, drinking iced tea that my Grandma Toodles had made for me. I didn't feel like flying, and there was nowhere else I wanted to be.

Time didn't seem to exist; I could have been there ten minutes or ten thousand years. Feeling nothing but happiness and peace, I rolled in the silky petals of my heavenly garden. And that was nice.

WITH NOTHING TO LOSE, YOU'VE EVERYTHING TO GAIN

I'm older now as I stare into a blue sky. Clouds float by and I smile, thinking back many years to my adventure in the heavens. The road since has been long and hard, but I've survived.

My kids laugh and swing as I sing songs on my front porch. Irene giggles as she comes walking out our back door with lemonade in one hand and a baby in another. We've made it through seven babies, two failed businesses, a stack of rejection letters from book publishers and record companies, poverty, disconnect notices, and every other imaginable hardship free-spirited, self-sufficient people go through trying to live a life on the road less traveled. But in our case, it really did make all the difference.

"Hey, Dad," says my oldest son Isaac, interrupting my thoughts. "Did you know that peanuts aren't nuts?" He smiles proudly at this fact. He's ten and reading a book on odd facts. In fact, he reads over a book a day at a high school reading level, all thanks to his mother's homeschooling and our collective sacrifice that allows her to stay home with the children.

"Look, Daddy," my nine-year-old Mary yells, and I look up to see her hanging upside down from the crossbar of a swing we just had installed. I smile and remember that a week before she was born, my first business failed and I was blackmailed by my two partners. Horror and joy – isn't life that way?

My eight-year-old Irene then walks over from the sandbox she'd been playing in and sits in my lap. She looks up and says "I love you, Daddy," As I rub her back, I think back five years and the pressure of dealing with two surgeries – one for her that we thought might reveal brain cancer, and one for me to remove a melanoma on my shoulder that if it had spread would have killed me in six months or less. And then there were the medical bills that almost bankrupted us and stomped on our dreams.

You see, the journey never ends. Since that terrifying July day, grace has saved me, and grace has taught me a brutal lesson. You wake up every day and battle to the end. You never give up. You fight on. In the years since leaving the Marines, I have traveled the world, been a professional photographer, singer/songwriter, business owner, college lecturer, magazine publisher, author, cancer survivor, husband, and father of seven. And I'm now able to share all this with our soldiers, Marines, airman and many others across the country struggling to overcome trauma. And just as importantly, people everywhere yearning to live life with passion.

But lying in that emergency room all those years ago I wanted to die. I'd never written a book or even tried. I didn't own a camera and knew nothing about photography. I was musically illiterate and couldn't play an instrument. I didn't even own or use a computer. I was antisocial and unloving. I had no idea who I was or what I could become. But I believed. And while this book and music have taken years to develop, I could never resist the burning desire to produce them and share all that had been revealed to me.

Samuel's story is my story. The fairy tales and dreams were the ones my mind created in order for me to survive all those years ago. It wasn't the Beatles who saved me, it wasn't my shrink, it wasn't my family, it wasn't an angel sent by God. They were all important, but it was Samuel, the little boy inside me who wanted to live and to whom God wanted me to listen, that pulled me through. I've let him fly ever since.

Whatever your situation, you are never too young and you are never too old to fight for your dreams. By facing your demons and examining the choices and trials of your life, day by day, eventually you will discover a peace that truly passeth understanding. There is a flame of life inside all of us; it can burn you up or set you free. I chose the latter.

WILDERNESS LAMENT

Looking across the wilderness
Afraid of why I'm here
To cage the beast inside me
The same that I hold dear

This ledge before me
My lofty perch
Temptation to paradise
Would death bring me enlightenment
Or dust, eternal damned life

And what of the rumbling hunger
Churning bile, a crumbling soul
I know not what to feed upon
Do I deserve to even know

These words of a man despairing
So sad, such lamentable pity
Crude poetry of simple cries
Lone dweller in his own empty city

That's my last tear falling to the sand
Tired of sinking
It's here I'll make my stand

And that which upon I feast

Manna sweet, the harvest of soul
Rapture found on the precipice
Of surviving forgotten hope

APPENDIX: AMP TEXT AND SONG LYRICS

Audio Motion Picture Text: This is the transcription from the CD Freedom Rising. Freedom Rising is both acoustic versions of songs and a spoken word recreation of my live speaking events. Freedom Rising is available on iTunes and my website, www.silouan. com.

The Child Fades Away

Descent into Hell

Sleep, My Dear

I Sleep with Demons

Let the Waters Flow

Tasting Freedom

That's the Man I'm Gonna Marry

Triumph, Failure, and Carrying On

Freedom Is in Us

My Treasure

South of Clarksdale, Mississippi

Freedom at Any Cost

AUDIO MOTION PICTURE TEXT:

The Child Fades Away

It was hot, dark, and damp. The hood over my head blocked any light except that glowing from the backlit dials and switches. A storm was coming, and the air hung thick with moisture. Sweat poured into my eyes, but my helmet's glare shield kept me from wiping them. I was uncomfortable, and everything was shaking.

Ten thousand pounds of thrust burned beneath me; twenty tons of metal groaned with the strain. The air conditioner wouldn't kick in until we were churning more air, so I sat in this furnace struggling to remain alert. Soon I'd be accelerating to over three hundred miles per hour. Everything seemed fine, but I was scared. Of course, I was always scared.

We were off, Lieutenant Skinner and I, into a storm we thought we could evade. But the storm wasn't the problem. Our problem was the fire – and the blinking lights and my paralyzed mind.

"Lieutenant Skinner, help me! Help me!" I waited to die.

And then my seat exploded, and I left the fire and the dying groaning metal. The air hit me like a wall, and I felt my body scream, and pull, and tear. Lieutenant Skinner flew by.

He hit a tree and then I blacked out.

Descent into Hell

I woke up in the ambulance strapped tight to a body

board. Everything hurt. My eyeballs hurt. The paramedics had cut off my boots and, thankfully, I could move my naked feet. That was a good sign. I probably wasn't paralyzed.

Road noise radiated up through the ambulance's chassis as we sped down the highway. Blinking my scratchy eyes as I stared up at the ambulance lights, my mind raced. What just happened to me? Where's Lieutenant Skinner?

The ambulance took me directly to a local hospital, where after being carted around for X-rays and a litany of questions, a serious-looking nurse walked up holding a plastic cup and said, "We're worried you might be bleeding internally. No one saw your parachute open so you probably hit the ground pretty hard. Try to urinate in this cup so we can check for bleeding. If you can't, we'll have to run a catheter." She patted my hand. "I'll be back in a few minutes."

I bore down, but my back just throbbed harder, and the cup remained dry. My concentration was broken when an officer from the squadron parted the surrounding curtains and with barely more than a "how ya doing" confirmed what I had already assumed: Lieutenant Skinner was dead. I'd been too panicked to potty; now I was just numb. But before I could reply, the nurse returned, the officer left, and the catheter was fed into my penis. I grimaced as the thin piece of plastic moved the wrong way up a very small hole. A grimace which turned into a scream as the tip of the catheter caught on something inside me.

Adding to my ordeal was the fact that before the ER could finish its tests, I was ambulanced away in haste to the nearest military hospital, all in the name of saving the government money. I can still hear the base CO arguing with the emergency room doctor. As the doctor tried to reason with him, the CO just kept saying "budget" and "he looks fine to me," and

129

when the ER doc stepped away to tend to another patient, I was carted off.

I arrived at the base hospital, and after a couple of questions and some poking by a nurse (the doctor was too busy), I was told that my back was probably just bruised and that I would be okay. I could even get up and walk around, if I wanted. This in spite of my continual pleas, "My back really hurts – are you sure I'm all right?"

"Yes," they insisted, looking at me like I was whining. "You're fine." So I followed their orders, and when I couldn't sleep I walked up and down the hallways. Little did I know that due to my abrupt departure, no records had been sent with the ambulance, and the staff at the base hospital had just assumed that I was okay, having been transferred so soon after the crash.

Assumed, that is, until the next day, when a nurse rushed into my room, her face flush with mild panic. "You need to stay in bed until the doctors get here with a brace."

"Brace?" Did she say what I thought she just said?

"You fractured your spine." She explained, "We just learned when the hospital called to check on you. If you fall, you could hurt yourself bad."

I closed my eyes as my body constricted into a knot of stress. But the nightmare had only just begun.

Months passed and my spine healed, but even though I kept complaining about my back pain, the docs kept telling me it shouldn't hurt. So I shut up, worked out through gritted teeth to get back in Marine shape, and prepared to fly again.

The day finally came, and in what seemed like a blink of the eye since the inferno, I suited up and strode toward a jet for the first time in over six months. I tried to walk tall, but images of a burning plane and the stench of fear filled my head as I moved across the tarmac towards jet 247. Thankfully, my instructor was patient and very encouraging. His confidence helped me focus on checklists and procedures until we were in the air.

Focused, that is, until a few minutes after takeoff, when we pulled some very low g's and I was pressed down in my seat. Because no other tests other than my initial X-ray had been run – again, to save money – no one knew that at that moment my spine would compress and pinch a nerve, and I would become incontinent, wetting my pants. This was all too much for me to handle, and the thin line between resolve and fear was crossed. Screaming into my oxygen mask, I begged the instructor to land.

With each passing day I slept less, the pain increased, and I began to eat painkillers like candy. When the base flight surgeon ran out of answers, I was sent to the Air Force's Wilford Hall Medical Center in San Antonio, Texas, for medical tests. Now everything seemed to be malfunctioning – my back, my mind, my bladder, everything.

At Wilford Hall I spent my mornings with a psychiatrist, the afternoons reserved for physical therapy. Mixed with the two were a myriad of tests to figure out the extent of my complications – sleep tests, pain tests, mental tests, muscle tests, and the worst, a bladder test.

I had once won the US Marine's Officers Basic School physical fitness award with a perfect score, the first in over two years. I had been one bad dude. Six foot two, two hundred pounds, a 355-pound bench press, and the endurance to rip off five-minute miles. But when you are lying on a cold steel table with a tube in every orifice of your body, including your urethra, any ego quickly fades, and you just feel like some pathetic lab rat.

The experiment to test my bladder function began, and the table rotated up so that I was standing about a foot above the hard floor. As if the tubes stuck in my penis, anus, and nose weren't enough, I could see a thick leather belt dangling toward the floor that seemed like it should have been strapped to me. But nobody bothered, and I was too freaked out by the impending test to speak up.

They would pump water in and out of my bladder via two tubes inserted through my urethra – yes, two tubes – while the tube that was snaked up my anus had an inflatable ball at the end and would test the pressure and functioning of my bladder. The test would be repeated, over and over. I'm still not sure what that tube in my nose was for; I can just remember gagging on it.

They started the test, and I could feel warm water running the wrong way through my penis. After a moment of excruciating pressure I suddenly fainted, the tile-covered concrete floor breaking my fall. When I woke up, a team of doctors and nurses were surrounding me. My heart had stopped.

A few hours later a nurse told me that I could go home. Still in shock that my heart had stopped, a huge orderly pushed me in a wheelchair to the front door, not even bothering to ask if there was anyone to take me home. Which there wasn't. I walked out of the hospital alone to my car, where I slumped over the steering wheel and wept.

Sleep, My Dear

She was a friend of a friend that I had met soon after arriving in Texas, and we occasionally hung out at the random party. There was never any romance, and we only spent one evening alone together, but it was an unexpected journey that provided some much-needed hope. For the first time I was able to talk about my crash and the loneliness I felt in therapy while my friends soared in the sky to someone other than my psychiatrist. She confided her failed marriage, unfulfilling career, lost dreams, and a childhood spent in a commune that started idyllic and ended a painful memory of communal sex. In her apartment drinking wine we got lost in conversation as the movie *Babe* provided background noise.

When the credits rolled sometime after midnight, we got into her Explorer and ran out for Crystal burgers. While devouring our late-night snack, we drove into the night as we dreamed into a future that now seemed a little more possible for both of us. Into the deep black, south Texas night we journeyed, two companions trying to replace painful memories with hope and possibilities.

After driving for hours we lapsed into silence and came upon a remote inlet where we boarded an auto ferry. Rolling down our windows to enjoy the breeze, the hypnotic rhythm of waves lapping against the side of the boat lulled me into a peaceful dream – peace I hadn't felt in years.

I Sleep with Demons

My heavenly trip into the night with Debbie D. was quickly overwhelmed by the demons of PTSD that began to attack me. Pumping gas at the convenience store around the corner from my house, the vapors hit my nostrils, and I was transported to the cockpit of a burning plane. As the fire raged, I screamed and pleaded, "Save me, God, save me!" But the flames just burned, while my skin melted and I begged to die.

"Sir, sir!" I heard a man yelling, and I woke from the

nightmare to see gasoline flowing from the tank onto the ground and over my feet.

Later that night I lay in my bed, filled with doom, rubbing my feet nervously together, where I waited for the demons to come again. I looked over at my clock and it read a little after 1:00 a.m. Exhausted to the bone, I rolled over to turn off my light when I heard something move in the living room. I called out and heard nothing, so I went to investigate. Discovering only my sleeping dogs, I walked back to bed. But again, just as I was about to turn off my light, I heard what clearly sounded like footsteps. Annoyed, I stomped back into the room and again saw only sleeping dogs.

So I headed back to bed. And again, as I leaned over to turn out the light, I heard the footsteps. This time I muttered, "What the hell?" and got up to go back into the living room when WHAM! The air grabbed and then slammed me onto my mattress, where my own hands clutched my throat and began to choke me.

My mind was a blur, my eyes sealed shut, my thoughts gibberish. A thousand pounds of force crushed me while I fought against my own hands. Struggling on the edge of consciousness for what seemed like hours, suddenly through the chaos a psalm echoed in my head. "I waited patiently for the Lord, he inclined and heard my cry." I focused on each word, and my head started to clear. Then, thank God, my hands fell away from my throat and the weight lifted from my body.

Lying in a pool of sweat, I slowly opened my eyes to see a demon hovering above my bed. Its face was covered with thin white skin, stretched tight. It screamed as I started to rise, and we locked eyes. I didn't back down, and, still screaming in a banshee wail, it flew out of the room.

"Woah," I muttered, then rolled out of bed onto my hard wood floor where I got down on my knees and began to pray. I felt a strange peace. Looking over at my clock it read exactly 3:00 a.m. – over two hours since the nightmare began.

Later that week I visited my psychiatrist, Dr. Germano, at Wilford Hall. Sleep was still an elusive creature, so around 2:00 a.m. on a Thursday night I went across the street to the Waffle House for something to eat. Weeks earlier Dr. Germano had encouraged me to keep a journal. While that sounded like a good idea, writer's block and laziness had kept me from putting pen to paper. But as I sat alone nursing a cup of a coffee, my mind became filled with images of a driving rain, and I asked the waitress for a pen. The words poured onto a napkin.

Took a storm
To crack the mortar
The stone, the aged clay
The walls I'd built to shield myself
From rains I feared to face

Took a storm
To clear the rubble
The remnants of my home
To find the lost foundation
Poured before I dwelt alone

And the waters flow
So today
I think I'll swim

In a Waffle House of all places, I had found the answer.

135

If I had the courage to lay myself bare, I could find peace.

Peace – what a sick thought that can be. It's hard to believe in peace when you're consumed with anger. And I was still angry with God, the world, family, friends, everyone and anything I could blame and make some perverted sense of my despair. In spite of having had the answer revealed, I was still cynical, still lost in the hopelessness of a soul ravaged by too many sleepless, nightmare-fueled nights and the horror of what now seemed like a wasted life. Had I been born only to die?

Let the Waters Flow

A burgeoning poet, the next day I fulfilled a lifelong dream. I walked downtown to an old music store and purchased a dusty Oscar Schmidt acoustic guitar on sale for $99, along with an *Easy Beatles* songbook. I headed home and went straight to my sofa, where I immediately began fumbling my way through *Please Please Me*. In the midst of the racket, I realized that I was smiling. Still alone, I was not lonely, and somehow I felt that the days and nights of praying down on my knees had been answered.

When the Marines determined I was beyond repair, a merciful flight doctor filed my disability discharge paperwork. While I was thankful, it dragged on for months – months where no one checked on me, and I wasn't required to physically report anywhere. Spending most of my time at coffee shops or home with my dogs, I idled away with no idea what I wanted to do with my life. None whatsoever.

By the time my discharge date arrived, I was ready for the road, and one thing was clear – I was ready to take off and discover a new life. In fact, I was thankful. The more I strummed and sang, the more I remembered a little boy who had written poems and composed simple melodies. As I grew up, the little boy had faded, but if I was to live, I had to discover him again.

In the end, it was pretty simple. I found a good home for my dogs, sent a few boxes of books and documents back to my parents, then sold everything else at a garage sale – except for my car, a bright red Porsche 944 Turbo. I was saving it for last. On the day of my discharge from the Marines, I met a flight doc at a motorcycle dealer, where he paid cash for my dearest possession. I then walked into the showroom, paid for a brand new Kawasaki KLR 650 motorcycle, and rode off into the sunset, hoping to find my destiny.

Tasting Freedom

I traveled for months, sticking mainly to back roads and small towns. Each day on the road seemed to reveal some new insight into my soul; fear was being replaced with freedom. Freedom that led me back home to Indiana and ultimately the college town of Bloomington, and a rendezvous with fate. I had discovered the blind hope of a child, and little did I know that it was preparing me for love.

That's the Man I'm Gonna Marry

Borrowing my parents' car, I drove into Bloomington, home of Indiana University, not expecting much more than a weekend of partying with an old buddy's little sister, and a chance to meet some of her friends before the semester began. I walked into her apartment on a Friday afternoon and to my surprise stumbled upon a pistol of a girl sitting on the floor in a pile of clothes with her shaggy dog. I introduced myself and quickly learned she was a biology major, ultimate Frisbee player, mountain biker, hiker, a prolific wearer of sundresses, and she was staying here for a few days in between apartments. A pistol, all right. I smiled and walked back to the kitchen for a beer, pleased at meeting my new friend. Little did I know that as I was sucking down a Corona, she was thinking, "That's the man I'm going to marry."

I saw her again a few nights later, when a group of us were at the apartment playing music – lots of Oasis, the Beatles, and the Pixies. I expressed some regret that while in college at Nashville's Vanderbilt University, I had never made the pilgrimage to Memphis to visit Graceland, and immediately people started to exclaim, "Let's go, let's just get in a car and go right now."

By the end of the night I was convinced to hit the road, but when the time came to depart, only one reveler had the gumption to go: Di, the girl I'd met on the floor. We drove all night and talked about everything from our favorite bands to the mysteries of the universe. We arrived at the parking lot of Graceland a little after 6:00 a.m., joined by a busload of Japanese tourists.

A few weeks later I passed through Bloomington again, this time on my motorcycle. Summer was fading, and I wanted to take a trip out west before winter arrived. I stopped by Di's place to say hello and discovered that she had been planning a trip of her own. She was going to take the semester off to visit family in Colorado, but as we discussed the possibilities, the journey soon became a party of two on the back of a motorcycle. The trip started with us sleeping in a rainstorm, and by the time it ended a little less than two months later we had sewn the threads that would seal our destiny together. Driving through the eerie desolation of the Badlands, we were hypnotized as we approached the Black Hills in order to pay homage to the immortals at Mount Rushmore and its cousin down the road, Crazy Horse Mountain. Camping at Yellowstone, we were woken each morning by elk nibbling on our tent. Far from civilization, we stopped in the middle of a sleepy Wyoming road to roll cigarettes and rest, having spent the morning in the shadow of Devil's Tower. Through twisted Rocky Mountain passes we rode mind-numbingly fast to escape winter's first snowfall. And on the rim of the Grand Canyon we woke each day to indescribable sunrises followed by treks through majestic Arizona vistas. Saving the best for last, we finished things up drinking tea with my Grandma Toodles in Mississippi.

Di never did make it back to IU, but ten years, five kids, and one wild marriage later, she's still the same pistol, never looking back.

Triumph, Failure, and Carrying On

Soon after I returned to Indiana from the motorcycle epic with Di, I met Chris at a friend's wedding in Virginia. He was tired of his desk job, and I was eager for another adventure. By the time we finished drinking a few pints at the reception, we had convinced ourselves that we could build a magazine empire. Of course, we knew nothing about magazines.

I'll spare the details – I might vomit to recall them all. But needless to say, the eighteen months or so of maniacally striving to establish "Bearfoot Magazine – Journal of Northern California Outdoors" was soul-crushing. I experienced the highs of gaining placement in all the country's Barnes and Nobles,

Borders, and London Tower Records, and won a national award for best start-up magazine. I was even offered my own outdoors segment on the San Jose NBC affiliate. All this while marrying Di and starting a family.

Then my paycheck bounced. The magazine had lost funding, and all I had was $300 in cash and a maxed-out credit card in my pocket. With little hope and even less money, we packed up and headed home to Indiana on Christmas Eve. The following afternoon, Christmas Day, we ran out of gas somewhere in Iowa. As the temperature dropped, snow fell, and our baby cried, we prayed that someone would stop on this lonely stretch of highway to help us. I can still feel the snow hitting my face, melting with my tears as I waited for help. I could not believe my world had fallen apart again, and this time I had a family to take care of. I had no plans, only a dim ember of desire and drive that, no matter what, I would hold on and keep stepping forward.

Freedom Is in Us

Since that Christmas Day disaster, we have struggled mightily to survive. There have been piles of disconnect notices, creditor calls, and hungry and hopeless nights, but we've fought on to live a life that we know is right. Once you decide to live free and hit the road, it's hard to turn back. We homeschool our children, and all that we can is centered on family and the struggle to be good and godly people. All while chasing the dream that life is meant to be a fantastic journey.

Listen to me, friend. Freedom is only a footstep away, if you'll strip yourself bare. Lose the crap and the worldly tools of addiction – TV, video games, drugs, and all the other shiny things that kill our humanity and turn us into sheep.

My Treasure

I've been at ground zero for all five of our children's births, the last four at home with midwives. Watching our kids grow I've learned that we are all given special gifts and talents to develop.

Isaac is a rock; he was born old. An altar boy since he was six, he can stand longer than most of the men. And he scored all but one of his peewee football team's touchdowns!

Irene is a ball of cozy with a mischievous smile that melts my heart. I love it when she sneaks into my office to share secrets.

Jude is ALL boy, ALL the time. He became attached to me at an age when most children are still clinging to mom, and he can make my worst day a good day when he says, "Daddy, hold me."

Our youngest, Maximus, while not talking yet, is fulfilling his name! The kid is a natural, doing everything early and always eager to jump in the fray.

And then there's Mary, second-oldest and first-born girl. Wherever she goes, sunshine follows.

South of Clarksdale, Mississippi

Now let me go back for a minute. I was in Pensacola, Florida, waiting for flight school to start, and decided to take a few days of leave to visit Grandma Toodles in Mississippi. Over a glass of freshly made sweet tea, she suggested I visit my second cousin Calvin, who was mentally handicapped and living in Rolling Fork, a small town hours away, deep in the Mississippi delta. "Sure, Grandma, that sounds like a great idea." I agreed, a sucker for my grandma and her sweet tea.

So on an oppressively hot August day I arrived to meet Calvin. My first impression was as bad as the long drive. Rolling Fork was a delta backwater, and his "school" was a crumbling brick structure with no air-conditioning. I couldn't help but think, who on earth would send someone here? But my disgust quickly disappeared as Calvin came bounding around a corner to meet me with a big, happy smile on his face, eager to show me his school and the mobile home where he lived. He loved Merle Haggard, Def Leppard, and race cars, and could not understand why he wasn't allowed to become a deputy and or go on adventures with the local National Guard unit. I quickly learned that Calvin was surrounded by people who loved him – the school staff, the local sheriff, a café owner who let him do odd jobs. Most everyone in town knew Calvin, and they were his family – a family whose love had transformed this poor stretch of Mississippi delta into an oasis of hope.

Years later, back home in Indiana after the magazine failure and in the midst of our family's struggle to survive, I decided that I wanted to be like Calvin. I wanted to help transform the crumbling and show people that love and purpose can be found anywhere. So I started visiting prisons, the poor, veterans, and anywhere else I thought I could find one person looking for a friend. And to tell you the truth, I've been given far more love and grace from them than I could ever hope to return. Thank you, Calvin.

Freedom at Any Cost

WHO AM I?

When I visit a prison I am always reminded of the remarkable humanity that can survive, and even thrive, in the most hellish of places. At one particular maximum-security prison, Pete would sit in the front row during my performances with a big smile and his undivided attention. Afterwards, he would always greet me with a kind word before he was escorted back to his cell. You would have never guessed that over thirty years earlier he had brutally murdered two women. Sentenced when the death penalty was outlawed, it was always a shock to remember that this gentle man had once been a cold-blooded monster.

In fact, everyone from prison warden to hardened inmate spoke of Pete's wisdom and peace, so during one visit I asked him, "How come you always seem so happy, Pete?"

"About twenty years ago, I saw a bird flying high in the sky through my cell window, and I started to pray." He spoke with a warm smile, "It taught me that whoever we are and whatever our condition, we can fly like birds if we give ourselves over to God. Ever since, my soul has lived outside these bars." I gave Pete a hug and said thanks. I wanted to say more, but before I could the guards were already walking him back to his cell.

Well, we've reached the end, and now I have a message for you, my friend. You were meant to fly, whatever your reality, whatever your hardship. No one owns your soul except for God. If you aren't chasing your dreams, discovering your purpose, looking to the heavens and asking God what he would have you do in that moment, you will always be enslaved, whether it be to ego, greed, possessions, pain, or hurt. You must strip yourself bare, simplify your life, and allow God to open your sails where he can lead you to a better place, a life of purpose and peace.

So many years have passed since I rode my fiery dragon – years that have taught me life is never easy when you are chasing rainbows. All too often the storms that precede them knock you on your butt, or worse. But in my darkest hours, when my deepest fears overwhelm and consume me, I remember freedom, I remember the road and my motorcycle, I remember that when you chase the light you are never far away from it, and I remember there is only one way we were meant to live. Free. No matter the cost.

SONG LYRICS:

Am I the Only One

Mary Is a Sunbeam

American Blues

I'm Gonna Run

Live Free or Die!!!

Hold On

Fly with Angels

Atomic Bomb

Debbie D

Flamethrower

Love Is Real

Purple Ponies

Vacation Home

We're Already Free

Am I the Only One

Looking at pictures of what our world has become today
Am I the only one who still gets down on their knees and prays

Looking at neighborhoods, churches built like castles
While poor people lay in the streets, soldiers scream in their dreams

    Am I the only one, am I the only one,
    Am I the only one, am I the only one

Where have the families gone, homes full of children laughing
Replaced with plastic surgery, homes built of golden straw

Where are the commune girls, hippies turning trees into dreams
All anyone seems to care about is the size of their shiny things

    Am I the only one, am I the only one, yeah
    Am I the only one, am I the only one

Am I the only one who still gets down on their knees and prays
Am I the only one who still gets down on their knees and prays

    Am I the only one, am I the only one, yeah
    Am I the only one, am I the only one

    Am I the only one, am I the only one, yeah, yeah
    Am I the only one, am I the only one

Mary Is a Sunbeam

Mary is a sunbeam, she's always been that way
Since she was two in a cowboy suit, singing her ABCs
And ain't that like a sunbeam, the melody that I sing
She spins around like a merry-go-round, never waiting for me

    Baby, come over, gotta have a reply
    Can't wait any longer, Mary, be mine

I was so busy chasing her blond curls I didn't see
All the times she was looking behind, the feelings she hid from me
And ain't that like a sunbeam, if you are too blind to see
She don't have the time to wait around, I'm gonna catch her and make
my plea

    Baby, come over, gotta have a reply
    Can't wait any longer, Mary, be mine

    And I will love you, Mary, I will build you a symphony
    To sing for you whenever you are blue, when you're away
    from me

Well I caught her on a rainbow, she was sliding to a pot of gold
She took hold of me and tightly squeezed, ruby lips said, "Baby, let's go"
And ain't that like a sunbeam, going wherever she please
I don't care, follow her anywhere, she's all that I want to be

    Baby, come over, gotta have a reply
    Can't wait any longer, Mary, be mine

    And I will love you Mary, I will build you a symphony
    To sing for you whenever you are blue, when you're away
    from me

    And I will love you Mary, I will build you a symphony
    To sing for you whenever you are blue, when you're away
    from me

The American Blues

A wide-eyed boy, playing in his lawn
Plastic soldiers all spilling their blood
Momma brings lemonade, she smiles then walks away
An afternoon of killing has begun

> She didn't stop to think, she didn't stop to think
> She didn't stop to think, that bullets sting

> What am I gonna do, got a case of the American blues
> What am I gonna go, got a case of the American blues

A college boy, can't listen any more
To teacher's talk of truth, they're such a bore
Professor says all that I'm gonna be
A blue-eyed boy making Cs

> He walks out of class, gonna be a bad marine
> Gonna fight for what is true, whatever that means

> What am I gonna do, got a case of the American blues
> What am I gonna go, got a case of the American blues

> I can't believe, what I left behind all means to me
> If I were you, I'd get down on my knees and pray for me

I couldn't believe when I felt the sting
How could this happen to me
Close my eyes and the pain goes away
Is momma waiting for me

> What am I gonna do, got a case of the American blues
> What am I gonna go, got a case of the American blues
> What am I gonna do, got a case of the American blues
> What am I gonna go, got a case of the American blues

> And I stop to think, is Momma waiting for me

I'm Gonna Run

I was ten, looked up in the sky, swear I saw a bird winking at me
So I climbed up on top of my house, heaven I wanted to see
I stepped off into the sky, sure that I could fly
But when I hit the ground I rolled up in a ball and cried

> I'm gonna run, I'm gonna find, all the treasure in my mind
> I'm gonna run, and I'm gonna climb, and I'll see you on the
> other side

Met a girl at a party one night, she sure looked pretty to me
She grabbed me, held me tight, said she'd been dreaming about me
I gave her everything, all my money and time
When I heard she'd been sleeping with him, I might as well have died

> I'm gonna run, I'm gonna find, all the treasure in my mind
> I'm gonna run, and I'm gonna climb, and I'll see you on the
> other side

Floated by for many a year, I was just killing time
Walked into a bar downtown, thought I'd have a pint and pine
Told Pete, known him for years, pour me a tall cold Bud
He looked me straight in the eye, said "Whaddya you doing with your
life, son?"

> I'm gonna run, I'm gonna find, all the treasure in my mind
> I'm gonna run, and I'm gonna climb, and I'll see you on the
> other side

Walked out of the bar that night, drove for days to the border
Met a girl along the way, she was cookin' for short order
I can't explain what I said, or what she seen in me
At dawn we were heading south, like that bird who was winking at me

> I'm gonna run, I'm gonna find, all the treasure in my mind
> I'm gonna run, and I'm gonna climb, and I'll see you on the
> other side

Light is fading, my mind slips away, looking back on what I've done
Everything is possible when I found the courage to run

> I'm gonna run, I'm gonna find, all the treasure in my mind
> I'm gonna run, and I'm gonna climb, and I'll see you on the
> other side

149

Live Free or Die!!!

Dark rooms and battered dreams, pretty girls just memories
Remember when I thought I'd be someone

Rains came crashing in on me, looking around but I can't see
I can't feel anything, there is no hope for me

>   I heard an eagle cry, she said, "Live free or die"
>   Ain't gonna fall on a deaf ear

Left my front door open one day, sold my radio, computer, TV
Bought a bike and then I raced toward the Texas sky

Smelled the grass, the dew, the trees, I just rode and rode, you see
Found a girl and I know she's gonna be the one

>   I heard an eagle cry, she said "Live free or die"
>   Ain't gonna fall on a deaf ear

>   Ooh, ooh, ooo, ooh, ooh, ooo, ooh, ooh, ooo, ooh, ooh, ooo

Having a beer in my big chair, I got children everywhere
Singing songs about the roads I done seen
When I hear the devil's song, tells me I'm just a little someone
I look outside and I can hear her singing to me

>   I heard an eagle cry, she said "Live free or die"
>   Ain't gonna fall on a deaf ear

>   Ooh, ooh, ooo, ooh, ooh, ooo, ooh, ooh, ooo, ooh, ooh, ooo
>   Ooh, ooh, ooo, ooh, ooh, ooo, ooh, ooh, ooo, ooh, ooh, ooo

Hold On

If you're like me, you stop to think
Your mind takes you back to places you don't want to be

Why can't we see, where our paths would
The choices we made should have been so different

      Hold on, hold on, hold on, hold on

I'm not alone, demons my companions
Can't open my eyes, I'm blinding

And I don't know why you stay with me
Don't you know, I'm lying

And I've lost truth, what's right or wrong
What does it matter when you're dying

      Hold on, hold on, hold on, hold on

      I'm gonna climb high, I'm gonna climb higher
      I'm gonna climb higher, look out below for me

Nothin' is harder than when you are trying to love anything
when your heart is dark
Nothin' is harder than when you are trying to love anything
when your heart is dark

      Hold on, hold on, hold on, hold on

Nothin' is harder than when you are trying to love

Fly With Angels

A blue-eyed boy, smiling with the sky
Thinking about my daddy every day since he died
I don't get down, when I sing my daddy's song
'bout angels in heaven, why don't you sing along

Fly away, I can't believe
The world looks so small from heaven
And now my dreams,don't seem out of reach
I'm ready to climb to heaven

Cause I'm not afraid when I die
Gonna fly with angels in the sky
I'm not afraid when I die
Gonna fly with angels in the sky

Everybody in town thought that I was crazy
When I packed my car for LA
But I wasn't afraid, I was on my way
Daddy taught me to sing

Fly away, I can't believe
The world looks so small from heaven
And now my dreams don't seem out of reach
I'm ready to climb to heaven

Cause I'm not afraid when I die
Gonna fly with angels in the sky
I'm not afraid when I die
Gonna fly with angels in the sky

Met her in an alley when I was beggin' change
Nothin' but a guitar to my name
But I played her daddy's song, she smiled at me
And through the night, you could hear us sing

Fly away, I can't believe
The world looks so small from heaven
And now my dreams don't seem out of reach
I'm ready to climb to heaven

Cause I'm not afraid when I die
Gonna fly with angels in the sky
I'm not afraid when I die
Gonna fly with angels in the sky
Gonna fly with angels in the sky

Gonna fly with angels in the sky

Atomic Bomb

Dropped a bomb, dropped an atomic bomb, on the schools that taught me
nothing
Dropped a bomb, dropped an atomic bomb, on the strip malls and
parking lots

This world is taking me away, I'm just part of the machine
This world is taking me away, I'm just part of the machine

> Run, run, run, run, follow the track,
> Don't turn around or you're sure to turn back
> Run, run, run, run, whatever you do, hold my hands, and I'll
> hold you

Dropped a bomb, dropped an atomic bomb, on everyone discouraging me
Dropped a bomb, dropped an atomic bomb, on everyone ignoring me

This world is taking me away, I'm just part of the machine
This world is taking me away, I'm just part of the machine

> Run, run, run, run, follow the track
> Don't turn around or you're sure to turn back
> Run, run, run, run, whatever you do, hold my hands, and I'll
> hold you

> I feel your skin brushing up against me
> Breathe a little slower now, let the world slow down
> Make it all feel better

Dropped a bomb, dropped an atomic bomb, on the homes lined up
surrounding me
Dropped a bomb, dropped an atomic bomb, on the world that is drowning
me

This world is taking me away, I'm just part of the machine
This world is taking me away, I'm just part of the machine

> Run, run, run, run, follow the track
> Don't turn around or you're sure to turn back
> Run, run, run, run, whatever you do, hold my hands, hold my hand
> and I'll hold you

Debbie D.

And the soul stays, when the child fades away
Check your heart today, lie awake and pray

Little commune girl, Debbie D., my Debbie D.
Release those britches, my eye shadow queen

Run cross the field, come bump with me
Wow, wow, wow

Then cross the ferry to the house of secret rooms
Where sweaty, naked mothers, holy fathers desecrate our tombs
Family tombs

Tell secrets shared with giggles, laugh aloud, drive along, along
Feed the belle till she's happy, dance all night, talk too long,
too long

And then Babe said, "Sleep my dear"
And then Babe said, "Sleep my dear, sleep my dear, sleep my dear"

Tell secrets shared with giggles, laugh aloud, drive along, along
Feed the belle till she's happy, dance all night, talk too long,
too long

And then Babe said, "Sleep my dear"
And then Babe said, "Sleep my dear, sleep my dear, sleep my dear"
And the soul stays when the child fades away
Check your heart today, lie awake and pray

Flamethrower

Heat rising up, metal surrounds me, this flying coffin headed for earth
Warning lights blink excitedly, a flamethrower is gonna eat me up

> This world makes you hard, turns you into cinder
> When life breaks you, fight back and charge

Flamethrower, shoot us from the dying plane, flamethrower, one survivor,
one dead
Flamethrower, kiss me with your flame, see a ghost in the mirror, I'm
to blame

> This world makes you hard, turns you into cinder
> When life breaks you, fight back and charge

Laid in bed for a hundred years, my mind sees demons, becoming insane
At the barrel of a gun, pointed at me, I decided to fight and rise from these
flames

> This world makes you hard, turns you into cinder
> When life breaks you, fight back and charge

> This world makes you hard, turns you into cinder
> When life breaks you, fight back and charge
> Fight back and charge
> Fight back and charge

Love Is Real

Some people think love's a mystery, but it seems simple to me
A girl who believes that I'll reach my dreams, a girl who will walk next
to me

Some people don't believe that real love is true, some people only settle for
what is easy
But when I see her eyes smiling at me, you know from true love you can't
escape

> Love is real, that's what this life is for
> When you can't see the sun, because your eyes won't open
> The thorn in your side is bleeding you dry, believe

Some people think love's a dying flame, nothing but a cruel memory
But when I feel her lying next to me, that's all the fire that I need
That's all the fire that I need

> Love is real, that's what this life is for
> When you can't see the sun, because your eyes won't open
> The thorn in your side is bleeding you dry

> Love is real, that's what this life is for
> When you can't see the sun, because your eyes won't open
> The thorn in your side is bleeding you dry, believe

Purple Ponies

Washed-out shadows, skipping away
Leading the child into night
Climbing the tower of pinks and greens
To find giant mulberry pies

> Dream away, dream, baby, dream, dream with me
> Dream away, dream, baby, dream, dream with me

Mermaids, fairies, lying awake
Purple ponies in your eyes
Running the beach of white sandy dreams
Drinking sweet pink cherry wine, wine

> Dream away, dream, baby, dream with me
> Dream away, dream, baby, dream with me, with me

Shine for me, my lemon tree queen
Take my heart tonight, tonight
Birds and trees, blue skies, blue dreams
Hold my hand tonight

> Dream away, dream, baby, dream with me
> Dream away, dream, baby, dream with me, with me

Shine for me, my lemon tree queen
Take my heart tonight, tonight
Birds and trees, blue skies, blue dreams
Hold my hand tonight, tonight

Dream away.......Dream away....

Vacation Home

South of Clarksdale, Mississippi, in the delta's deepest bowels
They sent Calvin Jones to a vacation home

I arrived on a hellish August day, inside the faces were deaf and dumb
They sent Calvin Jones to a vacation home

> He wasn't smart, so they sent him away
> He looked funny, so they lost the key
> Vacation home, what's it say about me

Welcome to the school for the retarded ones, then they took me to
Calvin Jones
He was in a room printing greeting cards
I walked in, his smile filled the air, he said "Cousin, sure glad to see you"
They sent Calvin Jones to a vacation home

> He wasn't smart, so they sent him away
> He looked funny, so they lost the key
> Vacation home, what's it say about me

I told Calvin I'd come from the Marines, flying jets higher than he
could see
Gave him my hat and he asked me to come see his place
Half a trailer was Calvin Jones, clean as crumbling steel could be
He had a Def Leppard record, and one from Merle Haggard
Magazines about racing cars and big trucks

> He wasn't smart, so they sent him away
> He looked funny, so they lost the key
> Vacation home, what's it say about me

Calvin smiled, this is his home, you see, cousin, think of me when you're flying high,
Calvin Jones smiling in his vacation home
I gotta go, he said, "I'll see you again, thanks, cousin, for coming to me"
They sent Calvin Jones to a vacation home

> He wasn't smart, so they sent him away
> He looked funny, so they lost the key
>
> Vacation home, what's it say about me

We're Already Free

Bursy, I understand, life ain't been easy
Sometimes it seems you ain't get no friends
Just a world, that ain't so grand

Bursy, like or not you're coming with me
Leave it all behind, there's so much to see over here
With me, as the sun is rising, over the sea
A white bird whispered to me, we're already free

Bursy, caught you staring again
You know regrets, like a steel cage
Girl, don't look back at stormy seas
All you gotta do is let yourself breathe

Don't look back on dirty days, can't go back now we're on our way, over
here
With me, as the sun is rising, over the sea
A white bird whispered to me, we're already free, over here
With me, as the sun is rising, over the sea
A white bird whispered to me, we're already free

Fear of failure, the world drags you in
What's real is the sun and stars, Bursy and me
I've seen you fall, scrape your knee
Don't let your fear keep your heart from me

Magic slippers on your feet, like a white bird you will be, over here
With me, as the sun is rising over the sea
A white bird whispered to me, over here with me, over here with me
A white bird whispered to me, a white bird whispered to me
We're already free

"Meet the man they call an Angel."
Jeannie Crofts, WISH-TV, Indianapolis

Silouan Green is a writer, musician, and creator of The Ladder UPP.

After breaking his back in a tragic jet crash and descending into a hell of insomnia, suicidal impulses, pills and post traumatic stress disorder, he took off on an epic two year motorcycle journey across the United States to escape his demons and find identity and purpose. From the rim of the Grand Canyon to the desolate Badlands, from the fields of Indiana to the western mountain ranges, he slowly found his purpose to help others out of the hell he had experienced himself.

While on this journey, he began to write music and a memoir of his recovery. In 2005 he began to share this work in prisons, and it eventually grew as a mission to find those anywhere who were struggling to find identity and purpose in life.

From the beginning of his mission, Silouan has focused on serving those in prisons and the military. Along the way he found that brokenness is something we all share. The key to better serving those incarcerated and our veterans is by making ourselves people who are on fire for life.

Silouan met his wife on that motorcycle trip, and today they have been married 14 years and have seven children! Silouan has created The Ladder UPP life skills program based on his own recovery. He travels the United States speaking and performing, and has founded a non-profit dedicated to building recovery ranches and reaching underserved populations affected by trauma.

Visit www.silouan.com to learn more and inquire about scheduling Silouan for your next event.

Made in the USA
Las Vegas, NV
26 October 2021